Rediscovering An American Classic
Essays on the Life of American Educator

Dr. Arenia Conelia Mallory
1926—1976

Dedication of Mallory Hall

Edited by Glenda Williams Goodson

With a Foreword by Bishop David Daniels
Chairman, COGIC Department of Education

HCM PUBLISHING
Lancaster, Texas

Selected Books by Glenda Williams Goodson

It's Been a Good Life! *Charles and Mary Beth Kennedy – Missionaries to the World*

I Want My Life to Reach Out and Touch Somebody!
A Biography: Gladys Venolia Johnny Ray Alexander Williams

Royalty Unveiled: *Women Trailblazers in Church Of God In Christ International Missions 1920—1970*

I'm So Glad I'm Sanctified: Wisdom Quotes and Treasures from COGIC Pioneering Women 1911-1975

Bishop Mason and Those Sanctified Women!

Our Mothers' Stories: History of the Department of Women with live interviews from COGIC pioneers
80 minute documentary on DVD

Books and DVDs may be purchased through the COGIC Bookstore, Amazon.com, other online booksellers or writing to glendagoodson@aol.com

HCM PUBLISHING
Lancaster, Texas

Copyright 2016 Glenda Williams Goodson

Photo credits constitute a continuation of this copyright page.

Rediscovering An American Classic: Essays on the Life of American Educator Dr. Arenia Conelia Mallory 1926—1976 is published by HCM Publishing

All quotations and references to Scripture, unless otherwise indicated, have been taken from the King James Version of the Bible.

Rediscovering An American Classic: Essays on the Life of American Educator Dr. Arenia Conelia Mallory 1926—1976 Copyright © 2016. All rights reserved. Printed in the United States of America. Because of the dynamic nature of the Internet, any web addresses or links contained in this book may have changed since publication and may no longer be valid. The views expressed are the author's only. No part of this book may be used or reproduced in any manner whatsoever without written permission except in case of brief quotations. For information address inquiries to HCM Publishing, 728 Sewell Dr., Lancaster, TX 75146

Cover design by Halo Graphics

First Edition

ISBN-10:0-9753342-8-X
ISBN-13:978-0-9753342-8-7

DEDICATED TO

The memory of Dr. Arenia Mallory and Saints College pioneers who fought for equity and justice in education and transformed untold numbers of lives

CONTENTS

[v] Contents
[vi] Foreword
[ix] Acknowledgements

[xi] *State of Mississippi House Concurrent Resolution No. 94: A Concurrent Resolution Commending Dr. Arenia Conelia Mallory, A Founder Of Saints College, For Her Outstanding Achievements*

[xiv] *SAINTS 101: A Short Course On President Arenia Mallory's Legacy Of Faith And Courage* Goldie Wells – Former President

[xvi] Introduction

[1] 1. *The History Of Black Education In The United States Is Complicated*

[11] 2. *Dr. Arenia Mallory Succeeds in God Given Assignment: A Model of Putting Feet to Faith* Barbara McCoo Lewis

[30] 3. *The Legacy of Two Institutions: Saints Junior College and Bethune-Cookman University Under Review* Willie Bragg

[51] 4. Arenia C. Mallory's Leadership Revisited: *Perspectives on Education, Politics, Culture and Community* Cynthia Bragg

[80] 5. *The Service And Sacrifice Of Women Going Into The Everywhere* June Rivers

[126] 6. *Arenia C. Mallory: An Example of Spiritual Prowess* Romanetha Stallworth

[140] 7. *Outlasting Life*

[152] The Contributors

[159] Selected Bibliography and References

FOREWORD

Rediscovering An American Classic introduces the reader to the phenomenal life and career of Dr. Arenia Conelia Mallory, a churchwoman, educator, women's club leader, and civil rights activist. Glenda Williams Goodson, the editor of this collection, authors chapters that open a window into the world in which Dr. Mallory lived, served, and sought to change. Goodson also weaves within the book recollections of Dr. Mallory by prominent female leaders of the Church Of God In Christ (COGIC), including Mrs. Barbara McCoo Lewis, Assistant Supervisor of the Church Of God In Christ's Department of Women, a space in which Dr. Mallory served with passion. These recollections offer personal accounts of Dr. Mallory's impact of women and men across the races. In addition to these recollections, Goodson shares the stories of an amazing group of women who interacted with or follow the traditions of Saints Academy and Junior College.

Rediscovering An American Classic chronicles the rise of Dr. Mallory from serving as principal of a struggling rural Mississippi school to her role as one of only two African American women to serve as president of a college in the early 1900s. This book displays Dr. Mallory's interaction with all sectors of society from the shanties of impoverished sharecroppers to the White House, where she was welcomed as a guest at the residence of the American president. We learn how Dr. Mallory used her influence and faith in God to educate over 25,000 students during her lifetime. The reader glimpses the life of Pentecostal women leaders who effortlessly cross racial, gender, class, and political divides.

Rediscovering An American Classic takes the reader on a journey from the sawdust tent meeting where Dr. Mallory was converted as a teenager to corridors of power that she navigated. Dr. Mallory, a "sanctified lady," addresses audiences in churches of various denominations, the National Women's Convention, and the Holy Convocation of the Church of God in Christ as well as the 10th Anniversary Celebration of the Founding of the United Nations. With grace and intelligence, she invites her listeners to "walk in dignity, talk with dignity, and live in dignity."

In *Rediscovering An American Classic*, readers meet the fine friends of Dr. Mallory. Her vast network of friends and associates speaks volumes about the respect that Dr. Mallory earned over the years. Bishop Charles Harrison Mason "calls" her to service in what he called the "little Africa" in Mississippi and appoints her the principal of Saints Literary and Industrial School, later renamed Saints Academy.

Mother Lillian Brooks Coffey, the second International Supervisor of the Women's Department, befriends Dr. Mallory and mentors her as churchwoman and national officer within the Church Of God In Christ. Mrs. Eleanor Roosevelt, First Lady of the United States during the presidency of Franklin Delano Roosevelt, champions Dr. Mallory and the Saints Academy. Dr. Mary McLeod Bethune, president of Bethune-

Cookman College, serves as a mentor and "second" mother to Dr. Mallory; they work together in the National Council of Negro Women, an organization in which Dr. Bethune served as the president and Dr. Mallory served as one of the vice-presidents.

Rediscovering An American Classic tells the phenomenal voyage of an amazing woman whose greatness extended far beyond the Church Of God In Christ. Dr. Mallory's impact reaches to various parts of the globe. She is a woman that people need to know and Goodson's book introduces them to this great woman, Dr. Arenia Conelia Mallory.

Bishop David Daniels
Chairman, Board of Education
Church Of God In Christ, Inc.
Henry Winters Luce Professor of World Christianity
McCormick Theological Seminary
Chicago, Illinois

ACKNOWLEDGEMENTS

Whenever I start to write, I know it will be necessary for me to ask assistance of many individuals. Years ago, I read Dovie Simmons and O.L. Martin's *Down Behind the Sun* after which I was honored to speak with both of them. When I first read Ms. E.M. Lashley's, *Glimpses Into The Life of a Great Mississippian and a Majestic American Educator 1926-1976*, I devoured it. As I re-read the story that she so painstakingly captured I felt as if I found a mine of information. And I had. I hope that this book validates each of their work and pays a part of the debt that is owed for their selfless efforts. Thank you Jessica Smith, Special Collections Librarian, Memphis State University, for your helpful assistance. Dr. William Dean is the pastor of the St. Paul COGIC. It is also known as the Mother Church as it was the first COGIC congregation established by Bishop Charles Harrison Mason. He readily filled in some gaps about the day to day operations of the school.

I appreciate each of the essayists – Dr. Barbara McCoo Lewis, Supervisor Romanetha Stallworth, Dr. June Rivers, Dr. Cynthia Bragg, and Dr. Willie A. Bragg. Dr. David Daniels and Dr. Goldie Wells have always encouraged and supported me on this journey to get these stories into the mainstream of church literature. Over the years, especially the last eight, I am comforted by the love of my son Anthony, his wife Tavisha and all my grand and great grandchildren. I also thank God for the prayers of my pastor (and younger brother), Elder Robert L. Williams of The Historic Open Door Church Of God In Christ, my mother Gladys Alexander Williams who is 94 years old at this writing and having been saved 78 years provides much wisdom in each of my endeavors. And I thank God for my Jurisdictional Prelate, Bishop James E. Hornsby, who has been a guiding hand in this part of the call of God upon my life.

Glenda Williams Goodson

State of Mississippi
House Concurrent Resolution No. 94

A CONCURRENT RESOLUTION COMMENDING DR. ARENIA CONELIA MALLORY, A FOUNDER OF SAINTS COLLEGE, FOR HER OUTSTANDING ACHIVEMENTS.

WHEREAS, it is the belief of the Legislature that outstanding Mississippians who have worked unselfishly for the betterment of this state should be recognized and commended for their works; and

WHEREAS, Dr. Arenia Conelia Mallory is such a person, having made immeasurable contributions to the people of this state, especially in the fields of education, religion and race relations; and

WHEREAS, Dr. Mallory came to Mississippi 48 years ago at the age of 19 and under the most adverse circumstances helped to found what is now Saints College in Lexington, Mississippi; and

WHEREAS, when Dr. Mallory came to Mississippi from Jacksonville, Illinois, and helped start Saints College as an outgrowth of the Church of God in Christ the school consisted of a two-room frame building; and

WHEREAS, at the beginning of Saints College in 1926 there were no plumbing facilities no electrical services, only three teachers for eight grades of pupils, and only two books for the entire school; and

WHEREAS, initially the college was funded to a great extent by money raised from a Gospel singing group formed by Dr. Mallory called the "Harmonizers"; and

WHEREAS, under the direction of Dr. Mallory the Harmonizers travelled the length and breadth of this land for 12 years during and after the Depression raising money so that Saints College might survive; and

WHEREAS, during the Depression the Harmonizers sang at Clayton Powell's Abyssinian Baptist Church in New York City before an audience of more than 8,000 and raised $15,000.00 for Saints College, a fantastic amount in light of those times; and

WHEREAS, through the determined efforts of Dr. Mallory, Saints College has grown to become one of the most respected community colleges in this country, attracting students from 30 states and several foreign countries; and

WHEREAS, from its humble beginnings in a two–room shanty, Saints College has become an institution with an enrollment of over 400 and a faculty of 36, 95% of whom have attained master's degrees and 4 of whom have Ph.D. degrees; and

WHEREAS, as a result of her works and accomplishments both at Saints College and in the furtherance of race relations, Dr Mallory has received numerous awards and citations from organizations all over the country and the world; and

WHEREAS, over the years, while teaching and leading the college, Dr. Mallory was able to advance her formal education, graduating from Whipple Academy; receiving a bachelor of arts degree from Simmons College, Louisville, Kentucky;

receiving a master's degree in education from Jackson State College; and receiving a master of arts degree in administration from the University of Illinois; and

WHEREAS, Dr. Mallory has received several honorary degrees in recognition of her tireless services, including a doctor of laws degree from Bethune-Bookman College; a doctor of sacred literature degree from Pillar of Fire College and Seminary in York, England; and a doctor of humanitarian from South Eastern University in Greenville, South Carolina; and

WHEREAS, Dr. Mallory, throughout her long and useful life, has shown herself to be a credit to her race, her state and her country;

NOW, THEREFORE, BE IT RESOLVED BY THE HOUSE OF REPRESENTATIVES OF THE STATE OF MISSISSIPPI, THE SENATE CONCURRENT THEREIN, That we do hereby commend and congratulate Dr. Arenia Conelia Mallory for her outstanding accomplishments in education, religion, race relations and service to her fellowman.

BE IT FURTHER RESOLVED That copies of this Resolution be sent to Dr. Arenia Conelia Mallory, Saints College and the Capitol Press Corps.

ADOPTED BY THE HOUSE OF REPRESENTATIVES
March 22, 1974
/s/ SPEAKER PRO TEMPORE
HOUSE OF REPRESENTATIVES

ADOPTED BY THE SENATE
March 22, 1974
/s/
William F. Winter
PRESIDENT OF THE SENATE

SAINTS 101:
A Short Course on President Arenia Mallory's Legacy of Faith and Courage

My tenure as President of Saints Academy was short, but Dr. Mallory's life and service at the institution were very much alive even in the 1990s. I first saw Dr. Arenia C. Mallory in the 60's when she visited the Holy Convocation in North Carolina as a guest of Bishop Wyoming Wells, who served on the Board of Education for Saints Junior College. Tall in stature and a thought provoking speaker, she made a great impression on me. During her preliminary remarks, she shared how she became a member of COGIC. Spellbound by her testimony, I was so inspired that when I became a teacher I wanted to serve COGIC with my educational gift. I also held a secret desire to one day go to Lexington, Mississippi to see the place that Dr. Mallory talked about and loved. That desire became a reality in 1994 when Bishop Louis Henry Ford and the General Board of COGIC appointed me President of Saints Academy.

As I took the reins of Saints, sixty-eight years after Dr. Mallory's leadership of the junior college, I found that her spirit was very much alive on the campus. As both former students and former teachers told me many stories of their experiences with Dr. Mallory, I vowed that I would do my best to build upon the rich heritage of sacrifice and triumph. Walking the grounds and moving through buildings she and the how things were when she began and how things had changed on the campus. I heard how she became teacher of the children, and changed Holmes County.

She came from Illinois to Mississippi, a place so different from her environment of origin, to discover a culture where Jim Crow was very much alive. She had been asked by Bishop Mason to relocate to help build an institution for the Saints to learn. I marveled at what the Lord had done through this great woman with extraordinary leadership ability and an abundance of faith. Moving through Faith Hall, I thought about how funds were raised to build by students she and Miss Lashley had taken across the United States to sing.

As I walked the grounds I would think about what it must have been like in 1926 when Dr. Mallory came to Lexington. I remember the stories Bishop Ford told about ringing the bell and putting out the buckets of water for the students to use. I thought of the struggle she must have had trying to educate the children and the adults. I thought of the challenges she faced as a female administrator. I thought about the task she had articulating her vision to the leaders of the church for advancing and expanding the curriculum from high school to a junior college. I thought about the genius she must have been to work with the white folk and the black folk in the community to get the help and support the school needed.

And as I walked the grounds I was grateful for the opportunity the Lord had given me to walk where this legendary woman had walked and as I faced some of the same challenges, I knew it was possible to overcome, because she had done it!

Goldie Frink Wells
May 2016
Dr. Goldie Frinks Wells served as President of Saints Academy and College, a branch of the Church Of God In Christ Education System, in Lexington, Mississippi, 1994-96.

INTRODUCTION

Stories are instructive in conveying culture and contextualizing historic events. Growing up in the Church Of God In Christ as one of twelve children of a church planter in the segregated South, my parents, Elder Joseph Robert Williams and mother, Missionary Gladys Alexander Williams, were thoroughly vested in the Church and adamant in teaching their children what it means to truly live out the sanctified life. The church thrived as spiritual authority and doctrinal exchanges through pastoral teaching poured from my father, a strong women's ministry led by my mother with much, much input from Church Mothers including our first Mother Dean Brown, dinners on the ground where we found emotional safety in the fellowship with others of like faith, with choir federations and revivals shaping our worldview. Overheard stories regarding the larger COGIC world from visiting ministers who, in the Jim Crow South, stayed in our home while conducting revivals for my dad were precious. We joined thousands at the Texas Holy Convocation in Waco where interweaved in the preaching and teaching of great leaders more stories of the healings throughout the Brotherhood, the work of foreign missions and the Church's educational efforts emerged. And reports and stories in the Whole Truth Newspaper were constant reminders of the work of Jesus Christ through COGIC Founder Bishop C.H. Mason,

National Overseer of Women and General Mother Lizzie Robinson and other pioneers.

Narratives of individual sacrifice, suffering and creativeness in navigating through obstacles to successfully achieve the completion of their assignment are vital and assist in moving the organization forward. Much of COGIC history is oral and that is one way I came to learn of Dr. Mallory. My mother shared stories of experiencing Education Day in the 1940s where the audience listened attentively as Dr. Mallory shared the struggles and triumphs of Saints. She heard Dr. Mallory's students, dressed in white, render presentations to the Holy Convocation. She also told of enjoying the ministry of song through the skilled voices of the Jubilee Harmonizer Singers.

Since 1997 I have taught the Lizzie Robinson Memorial COGIC Women's History Class in the Bishop O.T. Jones Institute of the International Holy Convocation of the Church Of God In Christ. (Bishop O.T. Jones, Sr. served as the second Senior Bishop of the Church Of God In Christ. During the Church's Annual Holy Convocation, the O.T. Jones Institute provides training to adherents over 50 classes addressing all aspects in the life of the church.). This book emerged from a question asked during a session on female pioneer educators in the Church Of God In Christ three years ago: *Since Dr. Mallory was so powerful and accomplished so much, why* don't *we know more about her and the Lexington school?* Just one question. My short answer: she was a tremendous force during her day and because prime space was provided for the school's presentations at every Holy Convocation, many knew of her and the school.

Afterward, the question provoked and poked me: Why *are* the

Achievements of one of the most successful academicians in the history of America, Dr. Arenia Conelia Mallory, President of the Church Of God In Christ premier educational institution, Saints College located in Lexington, Mississippi almost lost to history? Could recollections of paradigms of organization and strategic alliances to help students reach their highest potential provide a missing link to bridge the gap between baby boomers and millennials as COGIC transitions further to meet the needs of an increasingly global constituency? What is to be said of the audacity and downright gumption of one who should have passively accepted that COGIC students along with Holmes County Blacks only experience second class citizenship, now only mentioned in passing? Three and a half years later this book is my long answer. Before Dr. Johnetta Cole at Spelman, before Dr. Joanne Berger-Sweeney at Trinity, before Dr. Paula Johnson at Wellesley and so many other smart, ambitious, talented and gifted women, there is the hidden figure of Dr. Arenia Conelia Mallory at Saints whose story belongs in the center of the American epic. To define the individuality of Dr. Mallory and sublimate the essence of her personality, we must share the grand narrative of this individual who through faith in God, a determined will and a genius at networking and partnership changed the worldview of many and improved lives in Mississippi, the South and the nation.

The story of Mallory and Saints is melodramatic at the least and because of her seemingly indefatigable energy, high intelligence, spiritual fervor, silver tongue, great facility for friendship and marvelous egotism, Arenia Conelia Mallory was one of the most conspicuous women of her time. Her life requires further explanation and much could be written regarding her work in civic involvement, her influence in politics or women's social club work. Archives include her work for social justice as it extended to serving under Commanding General Mary McLeod Bethune as a Colonel in the Women's Army for National Defense during World War II. Black soldiers who took the oath to "support and defend the Constitution of the United States against all enemies, foreign and domestic" were in dire need of support as they fought for their country abroad while facing segregation at home. However, the current work, through the lens of foremost COGIC female thought leaders, intends to make Dr. Mallory's pioneering efforts in education easily accessible and demonstrate how Christ "in" her shaped the nation and the Church Of God In Christ. Indeed, Saints alumni working at high levels within the COGIC include or have included Presiding Bishop L.H. Ford, General Board member Bishop J. Neaul Haynes, First Lady Vanessa Macklin (the wife of current Second Assistant Presiding Bishop Jerry W. Macklin), Dr. William Dean, pastor of St. Paul COGIC (the Mother Church in Lexington, MS), Jurisdictional Bishop T.T. Scott, General Treasurer Bishop Samuel Lowe, Jurisdictional Bishop Walter E. Bogan. Other kingdom builders include televangelist Juanita Bynum, Pastor Maria Gardner and untold numbers of others. One of Saints' most prolific products is Dr. Leonard Lovett, PhD, pioneer President of Mason Theological Seminary. Dr. Leonard Lovett and others have written of Dr. Mallory's work and now research and study such as Dr. Anthea Butler's, *Women in the Church of God in Christ: Making a Sanctified World* and Dr. Anjulet Tucker's *Get the Learnin' but don't lose the Burnin' ": The Socio-Cultural and Religious Politics of Education in a Black Pentecostal College* shed additional light.

Rediscovering An American Classic: Essays on the Life of American Educator Dr. Arenia Conelia Mallory 1926—1976 includes extensive excerpts from a snapshot in time, *Glimpses Into The Life of a Great Mississippian and a Majestic American Educator 1926-1976*, a book by the exceptionally talented Ms. E.M. Lashley. Lashley served as Saints artistic director and was the energetic champion of the Jubilee Harmonizers who traveled with Dr. Mallory. *Glimpses*, like other hard to find Church Of God In Christ writings, is an important part of the Church's history and the musical Lashley describes Mallory's work in the elegance of a grand symphony. In order to provide those interested in African American and COGIC history opportunity to read original narratives, included are extensive passages from the book in Lashley's own voice. The limited editing I have done to those passages is only to provide clarity. My apologies for the quality of rescued photos.

Dr. Raynard Smith, Editor of *With Signs Following, The Life and Work of Charles Harrison Mason*, performed a yeoman's job in collecting and publishing essays from scholars. Following his example, the passages are interpreted through the 21st sensibilities of premier female thought leaders in the Church Of God In Christ.

Someone has said that fear, mated to power, produces intolerance. And although the education of Blacks during slavery generated terroristic acts upon discovery (selected bondmen were taught arithmetic for purposes of commerce), many were always fascinated with learning. To read was to discover a world away from bondage and many risked severe beatings at the least to embrace this skill. The first chapter, *The History of Black Education in the United States is Complicated*, places the complex educational journey of African Americans to overcome challenges, forge alliances and use their God given intellect within the framework of American culture. Years later, former Mississippi slaves still lived in grinding poverty due to their exploitation as sharecroppers. Arenia Conelia Mallory came to the fore of Saints Academy and dared to believe. Her mandate for those who would achieve success in spiritual and academic training, was to live their lives through the trinity of having faith in God, education and moral character. In Chapter Two, *Dr. Arenia Mallory Succeeds in God Given Assignment: A Model of Putting Feet to Faith,* Dr. Barbara McCoo Lewis, Assistant Supervisor, Church Of God In Christ Department of Women links Dr. Mallory's upbringing in her middle class household to propel her desire to utilize those principles to initially lift the children of her Church and her Race. With prophetic fire, Dr. Mallory seeds hope in Holmes County residents. She is unafraid to stand for equity, invites other denominations to send their children to experience the best education Holmes County had to offer and soon the demographics of the school include students from around America and the world.

Because of shared goals, many times the efforts of women having great minds coalesce. During the decades of the 1930s-1950s, the elder Dr. Mary McLeod Bethune served as a role model, encourager and second mother to Dr. Arenia C. Mallory and both had a strong desire to educate children. Dr. Mallory's heart for children was so great that when she saw bright children who could not afford the nominal tuition, she welcomed them to the school and allowed them to work for their tuition. As a result, many outstanding leaders were produced within and without the Church Of God In Christ including Bishop Louis Henry Ford, who Dr. Mallory met as a barefoot boy at a Clarksdale, Mississippi COGIC State Meeting. (Later, as the Presiding Bishop of the Church Of God In Christ, Ford would place proceeds from speaking engagements in a Lexington bank for the school.) Willie A. Bragg, Ph.D., Assistant Dean, School of Graduate Studies and Director, Center for Continuing and Professional Studies at Morgan State University outlines how the lives of two friends complemented each and were instrumental in maintaining their respective institutions. In Chapter Three, *The Legacy of Two Institutions: Saints Junior College and Bethune-Cookman University Under Review* she posits that the success of these great leaders was an outgrowth of their spiritual foundation. The essay also provides details of the older Bethune's struggle to establish and maintain her school while buoying Mallory to hold to her faith.

Bragg further includes information on the social activism of the women in their quest for gender equity and the role Bethune played in ushering Mallory into the corridors of American political power. As a result, Mallory's Jubilee Harmonizers gave a command performance at President Franklin D. Roosevelt's White House. She also worked as a Manpower Specialist and Consultant for the U.S. Department of Labor which brought needed visibility and funds to Saints.

The misinterpretation of separation of church and state notwithstanding, historically there has been a strong connection between religiosity and the political arena in the African American community. Whether clergy and other church leaders such as Dr. Mallory made proclamations from the pulpit or were public with statements critical to the wellbeing of its constituency, churches have served as havens, anchors, and mainstays while advocating advanced learning in diverse areas as a key to upward mobility. Political power and alliances are necessary and the case of Dr. William Dean, appointed the first African American Superintendent of Schools in Mississippi, offers a telling example of Dr. Mallory's use of political savvy to effectuate change. As Blacks began to vote, the White top administrators of schools wished to keep the status quo. Mallory, a member of the school board, stood and insisted that Dean be named Superintendent to transition Holmes County into the beginning of a new era in political equity. In Chapter Four's *Perspectives on Education, Politics, Culture and Community* Cynthia B. Bragg, Ph.D., Assistant Professor, Department of Sociology and Anthropology at Morgan State University sheds light on the fact that Bishop Mason, contrary to popular myth, was a staunch ally of education. She revisits Dr. Mallory's call to Mississippi from the COGIC founder and the way in which her partnerships with the Department of Women and outside leaders, grew the institution from "an acorn into a mighty oak" resulting in the transformation of Holmes County.

Since Rev. Lott Carey relocated to Monrovia, Liberia in 1822 and established the Providence Baptist Church, reported to be the first Baptist church in the country, Blacks have successfully fused evangelism, education and health care. (Goodson 2011:36). Today, global leaders such as June C. Rivers, Ph.D., Coordinator and then Director of COGICs Youth on a Mission since 1989, continue the legacy of enlightenment in America and around the world. Rivers' family has been intimately involved in World Missions since her grandmother's pioneering work beginning in the 1930s. Her father, Elder Havious Green, was also an activist who poured time and finances into missions. In *The Service And Sacrifice Of Women Going Into The Everywhere* in Chapter Five, Rivers provides an overview of Dr. Mallory's international travels resulting in the formation of an organization to assist in the travel to America and education of nationals such as the Honorable Alexander Gbayee, General Consul of Liberia and scores of unnamed individuals, many who returned to their homelands to lift their villages and communities. To shed light on the effectiveness of Mallory's efforts today, the chapter also provides the interwoven accounts of four women who continue the legacy to educate and inspire generations including Supervisors such as Lee Van Zandt, who had the privilege to learn directly from this giant of a woman.

In the Southern caste system, when being Black was treated like a disease needing to be quarantined (e.g., separate water fountains), Candace Laughinhouse states "as an upper middle-class, fair-skinned Black woman" Mallory exchanged a life of prestige to involve herself in activism in civic and educational arenas. (Laughinhouse 2011:12). These actions were motivated by her spiritual fervor. While she denounced conditions that would deprive individuals, especially Blacks in rural Holmes County, of inalienable rights of civic justice and equality guaranteed by the Constitution of the United States, the core element of her consciousness, indeed her spiritual perspective, caused her to work in very public places for the school she represented. Romanetha Stallworth, M.Ed., Kentucky First Jurisdiction Supervisor of Women, provides a thought provoking comparison of the Leadership style of Dr. Mallory and King Jehoshaphat in Chapter Six, *Arenia C. Mallory: An Example of Spiritual Prowess.* Stallworth explains how the Servant Leadership of Dr. Mallory required the same creation and implementation of vision, while setting and accomplishing challenging goals through prayer and faith.

Although Bishop Mason championed her cause the leadership of Arenia Mallory, a woman working in a man's world, was sometimes not welcomed. Once in General Assembly prior to Dr. Mallory's report on Saints, a delegate continued an attempt to get the Chairman's attention. Finally, Dr. Mallory asked,

"Mr. Chair, do you see that man?" When allowed to speak, the man stated "no woman is suffered to speak in public!" One wonders, after the demise of Bishop Mason, if the fate of Saints would have been different had the leadership (having an identical resume) been male. Saints closed after 50 years. However, one of the first items on the Church Of God In Christ agenda at the beginning of Presiding Bishop Louis Henry Ford's administration was the school's re-opening and with the re-opening raised teacher's salaries. Saints re-opened and closed several times after the demise of Dr. Mallory, however, her legacy did not die. Chapter Seven's *Outlasting Life* provide commendations from Mallory's 1974 Founder's Day celebration with testimonials from fellow college presidents, colleagues, and others. The reader also hears from students she taught to love God, be proud of their race, Walk in Dignity, Talk with Dignity and Live in Dignity. Among her "children" listed are those who worked in the space program to others caring for relatives to university professors. Because of Dr. Mallory's determination they received opportunities. This chapter also names some of the Jubilee Harmonizers, America's first all-female gospel group, and provides information on fundraising junkets to assist in keeping the doors of the school open.

The world owes a debt to every individual who has suffered to make it a better place and thinking individuals should not be deprived of valuable information relating to the Church Of God In Christ, which has some of the brightest minds in America. This offering allows others to discover who one of these individuals were but the real challenge is to document their work. This book is a part of my God given assignment to preserve and promote as one of the custodians of Church Of God In Christ history and relate its contributions to America and the world. It is my belief that in undertaking the difficult task of recreating, preserving and sharing history through the long forgotten voices of pioneer Church Of God In Christ leaders, this and other similar works will attract a new generation to appreciate the tremendous accomplishments God has caused to be completed through lives that would be used by Him.

Glenda Williams Goodson
Lancaster, Texas
June 2016

Chapter One

THE HISTORY OF BLACK EDUCATION IN THE UNITED STATES IS COMPLICATED

I just want to read from the Holy Bible before I die.
Female Ex-slave

During their introduction to America, Africans entered as indentured servants. A year before the Mayflower arrived in New England, a Dutch warship brought to the Virginia colony twenty African who had been taken as prisoners of war from a Portuguese caravel sailing from the Caribbean. When exchanged for supplies at Jamestown, they were given the same seven-year indenture contracts as many of the English who came to the Colony. (Phipps 2002:2). In ancient African kingdoms, some of these citizens practiced law through their court systems and having a history of great centers of learning, education was integral in their thinking. Indeed, Western Africans entering the New World may have known of the University of Timbuktu (which had an attendance of 25,000 by the 12th century) or, in the case of royal family members who were captured, those later seeking advanced learning may have attended. By the early 1600s, Puritans offered free education with the first formal school established in 1635. Those who first labored as indentured servants could have hoped to quench their thirst for knowledge in their new environment after joining others who served four to seven years in exchange for their freedom.

Generalizing the issue of education for Blacks in America is difficult. The present work is not the forum for a comprehensive examination of its rise of fall due to systemic racism, complicity of our own nor the color blindness of some millennials. It is understood that with the legalization of slavery in 1641, Africans were now considered property without human rights and slave masters understood their vulnerability of having an informed slave population. For the purpose of the examination of one woman's success in forging an institution providing academic excellence to students marginalized by poverty and systemic racism, we must grasp the underlying entrenched power and legacy as the stories here. The power of literacy was to be able to think, to imagine and perhaps to rebel against bondage. Across the South laws were passed making it a criminal offense to teach slaves to read and write. For example, in 1829 Georgia passed legislation making it a crime to teach slaves to read, and legislation and white attitudes discouraged literacy within Georgia's small free Black community. In the North Carolina the law stated in part

Whereas the teaching of slaves to read and write, has a tendency to excite dis-satisfaction in their minds, and to produce insurrection and rebellion, to the manifest injury of the citizens of this State: **Therefore, Be it enacted by the General Assembly of the State of North Carolina, and it is hereby enacted by the authority of the same,** *That any free person, who shall hereafter teach, or attempt to teach, any slave within the State to read or write, the use of figures excepted, or shall give or sell to such slave or slaves any books or pamphlets, shall be liable to indictment in any court of record in this State having jurisdiction thereof, and* *upon conviction, shall, at the discretion of the court, if a white man or woman, be fined not less than one hundred dollars, nor more than two hundred dollars, or imprisoned; and if a free person of color, shall be fined, imprisoned, or whipped, at the discretion of the court, not exceeding thirty nine lashes, nor less than twenty lashes."* (Raleigh: 1831)

An interview with 101 year old former slave Fountain Hughes sheds further light on day to day practices of his masters:

[W]e were slaves. We belonged to people. They'd sell us like they sell horses and cows and hogs and all like that. Have a auction bench, and they'd put you on, up on the bench and bid on you just same as you bidding on cattle you know...Didn't allow you to look at no book. And then there was some free born colored people, why they had a little education. (Interview with Fountain Hughes, Baltimore, Maryland, June 11, 1949 *(Transcription), master/afc/afc9999001/t9990A, Library of Congress, Archive of Folk Culture, American Folklife Center, Washington, D.C. 20540, afc9999001-t9990a)*

Times would bring change as Blacks attempted to transition from chattel to citizens. From the institution's beginning, some White colonists were not in favor of slavery, with Vermont being the first to abolish the practice. The Maryland Society for Promoting the Abolition of Slavery and the Relief of Free Negroes and Others Unlawfully Held in Bondage was founded in 1789. (http://www.historynet.com/abolitionist-movement) As the abolition movement grew and pamphlets with pictures illustrating the horrors of slavery made their way south beyond the symbolic Mason Dixon line in an attempt to influence public opinion against slavery, public demonstrations broke out. In 1829 a free Black, David Walker, published An Appeal to the Colored Citizens of the World in Boston, Massachusetts. He plunged ahead in calling for slaves to rise up against their masters and to defend themselves: "It is no more harm for you to kill a man who is trying to kill you, than it is for you to take a drink of water when thirsty." The power of the presidency at the issuing of the Emancipation Proclamation in 1863 (although it did not completely end slavery), further captured the hearts and imagination of millions of Americans including slaves. Former fugitives were further emboldened to write in publications and books regarding their bondage. Those publications were used as examples to demonstrate that Blacks were as capable of learning as were Europeans and their descendants in America, given the freedom to do so.

This freedom came after more than a half million died (some sources estimate over 700,000) during America's bloody Civil War. With the Emancipation Proclamation officially in effect Manumitted Blacks found a powerful ally in the War Department's creation of the Bureau of Refugees, Freedmen and Abandoned Lands (aka the Freedmen's Bureau). The Freedman's Bureau was created in 1865 to assist in bringing the newly freed slaves to full citizenship. In addition to providing basic necessities, other areas it assisted in helped former slaves locate family members, legalize slave marriages, settled freedmen on abandoned or confiscated lands (one senator linked land ownership with the Blacks' psychological and emotional stability) and promoted education.

From their first days out of bondage, freed slaves demanded formal education. When schools for freed people opened in early 1865, they were already overcrowded and within the year of Black freedom, thousands of former slaves crammed into churches or under trees to learn. While the Freedmen's Bureau did not hire teachers or operate schools, they rented buildings for school rooms and assisted Missionary Societies and Northern Whites, and provided books, transportation and protection against those who would oppose Black literacy. Blacks fortunate enough to gain an education took a proactive role in educating their brothers and sisters. Literate men who escaped slavery to enlist in the Union Army, for example, became teachers in regiments of Black men, and once the war ended, these same men taught in local communities. (Williams: 2005)

The Common School, embryo of today's public school, began in the 1830s when education reformer Horace Mann proposed a system of free and universal schools. Normal Schools began in the late 1830s for teacher training. The first state-sponsored Normal School was established in Lexington, Massachusetts in 1839. In 1868 General Samuel Armstrong (former Commander of a Black brigade during the Civil War), persuaded the American Missionary Society to establish Hampton Institute as an agricultural and Normal School for newly freed slaves. (Levin, Claudia Producer, *Only A Teacher*, KERA North Texas/ Hampton University www.hamptonu.edu/about/history.cfm. Phipps states,

The establishments of schools for African Americans was one of the most important outcomes of the Confederate defeat. In 1874 Wayneboro's "public colored school" did more than teach literacy. An inspection of its teachers and students displayed that "in arithmetic, geography, grammar [and] penmanship few schools in the land would make a better show. (Phipps 2002:5).

Black women played a major role in education. By the early twentieth century, seventy-five percent of public school teachers were female. Their efforts resulted in a measure of success as African Americans transitioned in assimilating into mainstream America, yet the majority of Black schools relied on used textbooks and equipment, after their white counterparts discarded them. African-American teachers were usually paid significantly less than their white peers and their civil rights were often compromised. (For instance, in a later era, Levin states that belonging to the NAACP could be grounds for dismissal and southern affiliates of the National Education Association denied Black teachers membership.)

Historically, the church, the family and the schools have worked together and served as anchors of Black communities. Clergy believed that if America was indeed one nation under God she should reflect biblical principles and, because of their visibility in the community, spoke boldly in fighting for justice. One of those principles was the freedom to learn. Tucker writes

Black churches formed the core of black educational philanthropy in the South. In poorer communities, black church-run schools were the only schools available. Before (and after) universal education was put into place in 1870, church-run schools filled the void. Some of the church-run schools became colleges. Well-known Spelman College got its start in the basement of Friendship Baptist Church in Atlanta. Wilberforce University (1865) supported by the AME Church, Morris Brown College (1881) and Livingstone College in 1879 were both Church established. (Tucker 2009:64)

In Mississippi, education for Negroes was stringently opposed. White school boards seldom hired enough teachers for African American students, and the teachers they did bother to hire were almost never college graduates. In one county, there were only three teachers for a population of 350 students. During the harvest season, officials in Delta schools refused to open until all harvests were gathered causing some schools to reopen as late as mid-November. Some Blacks answered the issue with boarding schools such as the Christian based Piney Woods School established in 1909. Mississippi's COGIC, with its unique doctrine, would also respond to families seeking a quality education for the children of its constituents. COGIC was born in the pain of conflict and has a legacy of great achievement amidst turmoil and challenge. Some thirty two years after the American Civil War, the Church was born (1897) under the leadership of former Baptist ministers Rev. Charlies Price Jones and Rev. Charles Harrison Mason. Jones and Mason, believing sanctification important to the Christian life, preached the second blessing and were later joined by other Baptist ministers including Rev. John Jeter and Rev. W.S. Pleasant. Tensions grew as these militant preachers espoused holiness and sanctification resulting in the right hand of fellowship being withdrawn by their Baptist brethren. Those excommunicated believers formed COGIC as a holiness church in Jackson, Mississippi. In 1906 COGIC leader Rev. C.P. Jones directed Rev. C.H. Mason, Rev. D.J. Young, and Rev. J.A. Jeter West to explore the unusual and supernatural occurrences in Los Angeles. It was while attending the Azusa Street Revival that Charles Harrison Mason received the Baptism in the Holy Ghost with the biblical sign of speaking in tongues. As a result of doctrinal differences surrounding initial evidence of Holy Ghost Baptism (speaking in tongues) between groups led by Rev. C.P. Jones and others led by Rev. C.H. Mason, the right hand of fellowship was withdrawn and COGIC was then reorganized as a Holiness-Pentecostal organization.(Goodson 2011)

The newly formed Holiness-Pentecostal church was met with

skepticism and disdain by many. COGIC members, along with their children were ostracized. Due to the hostile environment, a space for their children was required. Miss Pinkey Duncan was the first known foot soldier to attack ignorance when she started her educational pursuits in the basement of St. Paul Church Of God In Christ, Lexington, Mississippi. Sis. Duncan was undaunted by the mud floors. Bishop Charles Harrison Mason encouraged the beginning of what was then known as the Saints Home Industrial School in 1918. He was pastor at St. Paul and his children were the first students along with the Cooper children (Goodson 2002:20) Duncan understood that those children of the families who joined the new church were persecuted because of their religious beliefs and required a sensitive hand in spiritual and educational development. Professor James Courts of Lexington, Mississippi, a county schoolteacher, offered to help Sister Duncan with the work. In 1919, the State Board appointed him to the position of principal, which he held from 1919 until his death in 1926.

The vision of Bishop Charles Harrison Mason, to take the message of Jesus Christ into the everywhere, reached Illinois where Arenia Conelia Mallory was saved. Bishop Mason seemed to have an unusual knack for discovering individuals with keen abilities. After identifying them, he would next mentor those individuals to transform the development of the Church Of God In Christ into the premier organization that God promised him upon his acceptance of his call. These individuals in turn respected their leader and worked untiringly for the cause of Christ because of Mason and like followers. By the time Mallory met Mason her intent was to travel to Africa to serve the Lord Jesus among her brethren there. Mason saw something in Mallory. According to her testimony, (at his funeral during the 1961 Holy Convocation in Memphis) his message had a profound impact in the direction her life would take.

The best friend I ever had was Bishop Charles Harrison Mason. He believed in me when I didn't believe in myself. He helped me to hope when I had done hoping. He forgave me as a father for my faults. And he demanded that men and women give me a chance to build an institution for the church that he gave his life for. He sent his own children there when we didn't have an electric light, nothing but mud. He believed in Saints Industrial and Literary school. He visited it several times a year. And in his active years he met every board meeting. When there would be instances where perhaps our misunderstandings would have closed its doors he would call us on our knees and keep us there five and six hours.

Saints Junior College children number in the hundreds throughout the world today and their children that knew him loved him. And I am here today because he taught them and he taught me that the prayer of faith shall save the sick. And so a child came and knelt by the bed from far away Africa when I had given up hope of coming at this time and when that child, Abraham Brown, a young man from Africa got through praying I got up. For I seem to hear him say the prayer of faith shall save the sick. And when Sis. Elsie Shaw called on the telephone minutes later I said I'll be there by faith tomorrow.

I was taught faith through the church and the doctrine that he preached. I was taught righteousness. If I am lost it is my own fault for I have sat at the feet of Gamaliel or a greater than Gamaliel.

Saints Junior College with its hundreds of children yet unborn at this time salutes our general, our loved one, as we bid him farewell until the morning breaks. And on that morning we pledge that when you stand with the apostles to judge the world as I believe you will, there will be thousands of children coming up out of Saints Junior College and their children's children because you lived and because you loved and because you wanted a school for the church. And now farewell father, farewell.

Mallory never travelled South until Bishop Mason inspired her to come and see what she could do for the deprived and disadvantaged people in the rural area of Mississippi. She journeyed to Lexington and worked with Professor Courts. After his death, she was appointed president, not without some resistance; enrolment was opened up to all, and denominations including Catholics swelled the student body to increase from 10 to 350 rapidly.

In the following chapters, an essay will be written by one of the scholars identified after which an excerpt from Mrs. Lashley's book will be provided (in italics). Many times photos are not included in a compilation of essays, however, because 21st century readers must understand the sheer magnitude of what Dr. Mallory accomplished in the 50 years she stood at the helm of Saints, the editor determined that rare photos of the school and activities add value to the work.

Chapter Two

PUTTING FEET TO FAITH:
Dr. Arenia Mallory Succeeds In God Given Assignment

Barbara McCoo Lewis

Keep your head up, throw your shoulders back and reach for the stars. If you keep your hands in God's hand, you can make it. Don't let anyone tell you can't make it. Just Walk in dignity, Talk with dignity, and Live in dignity. Be proud of your race and love God. – Dr. Arenia Mallory

In the early 20th century women who were Black, for the most part, were not expected to achieve great dreams. Yet they did. History speaks to us of women who felt the responsibility of assisting the Race in their efforts to reach the goals of Americans—life, liberty and the pursuit of happiness—for everyone. And with that expectation, came responsibility which the women used to uplift the Race in every sphere of life. Born free, Rosetta Douglass Sprague was the first child of Frederick Douglass, the famous ex-slave and Abolitionist. As she grew her father cautioned her "Daughter, I am sending you to school for your benefit; see to it that you are punctual in attendance, that you do not offend in your demeanor and cope with the best of them in your lessons—and await the results." Later she would write that women, especially those having of privilege of education, "would in every city, town and village, where any number of the race reside…form aid societies for the maintenance of kindergartens and industrial schools…".

This is the worldview of the talented tenth who spread the message of racial uplift. One of those daughters, Arenia Conelia Mallory, should be extolled as a role model of courage, determination and a faith that could not be diminished. She believed that in having faith in God, education and building moral character there was no defeat. As a young woman she made a profound impression on me as I observed her. At every Church Of God In Christ Holy Convocation "Education Day" was arranged by Mother Lillian Brooks Coffey to raise funds for the school.

Education Day was special. Each year the people wanted to hear from Dr. Mallory and the students at Saints. They wouldn't leave but listened. The students sang and at night someone from the school would preach. (Supt. William Dean taught at Saints and briefly served as President upon its reopening by Bishop Ford.)

Mother Coffey did this to decrease need for emergency assistance, and Dr. Mallory presented the accomplishments of *our* school down behind the sun which, under her steady hand, evolved from a rural industrial school to the accredited (1954)

Saints Junior College. As students took the stage, I saw well trained, well behaved and confident young people. They may have hailed from Mississippi or Maryland County in Liberia, West Africa. Whether it was the soul stirring sounds from her Jubilee Harmonizers under the direction of Music Director Lashley (the group not only sang to raise funds across the country but also had a command performance in President Franklin D. Roosevelt's White House) or the elocution of word performances, the programs were carried out with precision and grace. Mallory influenced COGIC through the training of future pastors, evangelists, missionaries, bishops, supervisors and international missionaries. And in the world outside COGIC, her direct societal impact caused others to lift as they climbed in areas of education, medicine, entrepreneurship and science. She watched *us* watch *their* performances with pride. She loved them, she mentored them and she believed in them.

Dr. Mallory was sold out to keeping her God breathed assignment. This essay presents the story of a phenomenal woman who despite heavy odds persevered to provide "her children" with a first rate education that resonated with the admonition that they "walk in dignity, talk with dignity, and live in dignity." I am blessed to say that she was one of my mentors. I will forever be thankful that Dr. Arenia Conelia Mallory passed through my life.

THE EARLY YEARS

The year Arenia Mallory was born her famous mentor, Mary McLeod Bethune, founded a college in Daytona Beach, Florida. The lives of these women would be linked as they were hailed as great educators. At the turn of the century on

December 25, 1904 in the city of Jacksonville, Illinois Mr. Edward Mallory and Mrs. Mazy Mallory became the parents of  Arenia Conelia Mallory. Little did they know that their daughter would change the educational landscape of Mississippi along with the lives of thousands through a combination of fearlessness, determination and faith in Almighty God. Her early life was one of privilege. Her father was a businessman and there were musicians and entrepreneurs counted among family members. Emblematic of their status as members of the Black middle class were the facts that her mother was the first female African American Italian harpsichordist in the United States. Family members were also vaudevillians, performing in variety shows across the country. According to Tucker, Mallory's graduation from the Whipple Academy of Music provided further evidence of their status:

Her father owned a store before his death during Mallory's senior year of high school. Mallory's brother Frank flew planes for recreation, a hobby reserved for those with means. In addition to working in the family business, the Mallory men formed a band that gained a national reputation. Arenia's brother Eddie married the blues singer Ethel Waters in the 1940's, solidifying the family's position in the Black middle class. (Tucker 2009: 63-64)

Tucker further adds that as a member of the Black elite, education and service were mainstays in the life of the family. Mallory joined others in serving the less advantaged and formed a reading program for disadvantaged girls. She also worked as a recreational director for a Baptist run orphanage in Chicago.

Biographers Dovie Simmons and Olivia Martin report Mallory being introduced to the Church of God in Christ at age 16 when, with a group of friends, traveled to a tent revival intending to ridicule the 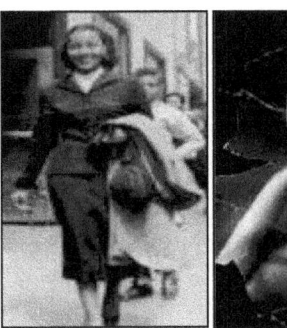  saints. It was there she was saved. Her family was horrified that she joined the sanctified church and an ultimatum was issued—leave the church or leave home. Although her mother would later become one of her chief supporters, after graduating high school, Mallory began to travel with a group of ministers and missionaries of the Church Of God In Christ.

Because her family believed in the power of education and in spite of any obstacles to higher attainment of Blacks, Mallory would hold dear the importance of this area of life. Soon after slavery, educational institutions were established for Blacks. The idea for such a school in Louisville, Kentucky was introduced four years after slavery by a group of Black Baptists but was not realized until 1879 when the Kentucky Normal Theological Institute (Simmons College) opened (http://www.simmonscollegeky.edu/brief-history/). It was there Mallory earned a B.A. in Education (www.lrc.ky.gov/record/14RS/HR90/bill.doc). In 1936 she received a Master's Degree in Education from Jackson College, Jackson, Mississippi. While leading Saints she commuted between Mississippi and Illinois, receiving a Master of Arts Degree in Administration from the University of Illinois in 1950 (Lashley:1977).

Mallory, like many strong female leaders of her day, was married briefly but divorced. The couple had one daughter, Andrea M.E. Clemmons. Andrea would serve as Director of Saints College Head Start Center (1965-1969) and Director of Admissions (1973-1976).

A DEEP DETERMINATION

Bishop Mason and the saints had big dreams for the Saints Industrial School. While in the early 20th century, the Church Of God In Christ was an anomaly in the religious world, the saints were like other church members who were progressive in their thinking. The children of the saints needed an institute of learning. One of the saints, Miss Pinkey Duncan established the first classes and the school was soon relocated to the basement of the St. Paul COGIC, founded and pastored by Bishop Mason. The floor was mud. Because of religious prejudice concerning the sanctified church, the school would also meet the goals for providing a safe environment where students would be free from harassment for their peculiar style of worship or their doctrines. Saints Industrial, owned by the Church Of God In Christ and chartered by the State of Mississippi in 1918, would go on to serve the saints by providing an excellent education as well. Professor James Courts of Lexington, Mississippi, a county schoolteacher, offered to help Sister Duncan with the work. In 1919, the State Board appointed him to the position of principal, which he held from 1919 until his death in 1926.

Mallory set her goal to travel to Africa to serve her people on the great continent. However, upon meeting Bishop Mason, he persuaded her to use her talents in Mississippi where he had established a school. Young, intelligent and intrigued, Mallory dismissed Africa preparations and agreed to serve as a music teacher under the leadership of Professor Courts. Upon her arrival she was shocked to see the frame building erected on brick stilts and surrounded by cotton fields. Yet, she decided to remain.

At the site of a little school (owned by a Local Church of God in Christ) Miss Mallory found a little frame building erected on brick stilts, a mile and a quarter from the heart of the town of Lexington, surrounded by cotton rows, and located on a dark muddy road. The equipment included a few homemade benches, two or three lamps and a few old iron beds. (Brown:142)

Soon after her arrival Professor Courts died and Bishop Mason named her Principal. She worked hard to overcome negativity both within the church and without. Without because she entered the Southland as a Northerner who may bring new ideas to upset the community's social mores, and she was resisted from within the church because she was female.

Dr. Mallory also believed in the power of strategic partnerships and saw possibilities of galvanizing the community—the religious community and poor sharecroppers—to educate those who would be informed and effectuate change. Additionally, Mallory had confidence that providing education for the children of the saints as well as sharecropper's children would promote a broader understanding of the sanctified church while serving as a venue for the upward mobility of Blacks in Holmes County, Mississippi. The task would be daunting but Mallory was firm in her belief that the God she served would make a way for her to accomplish her assignment. She proceeded to develop an expanded curriculum for the school and invite other denominations to send their children. Soon the student population swelled to 350 and included Catholics.

The issue of funding was problematic yet Mallory had a deep determination for the school to succeed. Some students such as future General Board member Bishop Frederick Washington had the means to pay room and board which by 1954 was $.25, $.50 or $1.00. (Tucker: 2009). Most students worked in gardens to raise their food. She persuaded individual church leaders to become vested in the school's success. Many responded, showing their faith in Mallory's leadership, by purchasing needed equipment such as refrigerators or even providing funding for the erection of buildings, which bore names of benefactors (e.g., [Bishop] O.M. Kelly Chapel, [Supervisor Mattie] McGlothen Guest House, [National Mother] Lizzy Robinson Dining Hall, [Bishop] B. S. Lyles Auditorium and Alumni Library, [Supervisor] Gamble Rice Hall for High school boys, [Bishop] F.D. Washington Residence Hall for College Young men). Bishop Mason as well as the Department of Women encouraged the support of the school and gave of their substance to keep the school current. In fact, the mission statement of the first Women's Convention held in 1951 in the city of Los Angeles led by its founder, International Supervisor Lillian Brooks Coffey included that the financial support of missions and education would be of prime import to the convention's success.

FAITH SAYS THERE IS NO DEPRESSION IN GOD

In the 1930s America and the world were in the throes of the Great Depression. By 1931 the number of Americans out of work has risen to a level of 6 million. In Mississippi 40,000 farmers would lose their land because they were unable to pay their taxes. Axiomatically, when the larger society coughed, the average community of color caught pneumonia. When Black

Faith Hall

farmers, as well as Whites, lost their land in Mississippi, there was nowhere to go. Sheriffs evicted them from the land and they did not have the necessities of life. Bread lines and soup kitchens opened to feed the homeless. Of course, saints in the 23 year old Church Of God In Christ as well as the Saints Industrial School were also affected by the economy. Teachers who were barely paid, now waited months on end for any sustenance.

Dr. Mallory put feet to her faith and taught staff and students to do the same. One of the most telling stories of Dr. Mallory demonstrates her faith in prayer to God. The older saints admonished the church to "pray through," that is seek the will of God until an answer is given from heaven. In the *Glimpses* excerpt, the reader will appreciate Mallory leading the school in prayer after a building burned. After laboring in prayer for hours Mallory received her answer when the Spirit bade her to go to New York and she would receive the funds. Despite the country suffering from the Great Depression, Mallory told students and staff that there was no depression in God.

Therefore, in June of 1931 she took a group, including the Harmonizers, to New York informing the contractor he would have his money for the building upon their return. Mallory and Music Director Lashley believed that God would use the gifted and anointed Harmonizers, the first female Black gospel group in the country. Mallory's sister-in-law internationally acclaimed singer, Broadway star, and Academy Award nominated entertainer Ethel Waters (1896–1977) reflected fondly on the talent of the young girls in the Jubilee Singers in her autobiography, *His Eye is on the Sparrow*.

When the girls sang there was nothing between them and their God. There was nothing to stop their voices, rich and full of heart, from reaching him. These were voices untampered with, and they were raised in song not to impress people or to earn money. They were singing to express something they felt and that they never could say in words if they went to all the Vassar's and Howard Universities on earth. (Tucker:2009)

As Lashley relates, at the end of the season of travel in the New York area during the worst Depression the world had seen, Mallory and the students returned with $8,000 (some accounts report $15,000) to build *Faith Hall*.

MAKING THE MOST OF HER TIME

At the close of the Mallory era, it was reported that more than 25,000 students had matriculated through Saints. It was no small task but Dr. Mallory knew how to work with almost everyone as she focused on her assignment. Among those giving tribute to the work of her hands were college and university presidents, political figures and individuals from every spectrum of corporate and business life.

Women who would succeed in life necessarily have to have strong personalities. While tolerating belittlements graciously, Arenia Mallory was said to be tough and circumstances would prove it. Bishop Mason and Azusa Street leader Apostle W.J. Seymour before him, envisioned a multiracial body of believers working together for the cause of Christ's kingdom. Mallory faced some tough decisions in this area. When three White teachers ventured South to begin service at Saints, it is recorded that local segregationists ordered her to rid the school of them. When she would not comply, segregationists threatened her with lynching. It was only when White businessmen came to her one night and pleaded with her not to be the cause of a bloodbath in the area that she relented. Other examples of her strength were more humorous. One respondent, Kevin Wilson, Sr., recalled a day as he threw rocks at the bell that signaled campus activities, a large shadow loomed behind him.

I was afraid to look up because I was afraid of that lady and didn't like her personally. She said, you like to ring the bell? Then I want you to ring it every day for a month. The first bell rang early for the Morning Prayer and I had to get up by 4:45 a.m. I had to be at my post!

She cared for us and educated us. We participated in English tournaments, music tournaments...I was taking calculus in 10th grade. She said she was NOT preparing us for a high school diploma. She was preparing us for life. And on my worst uncivilized day, I walked in dignity, talked with dignity and lived in dignity. I wouldn't trade going to school there for anything.

Black and white residents as well as those from the North began to note the success of the school and some sent their children. During the 1970s even two Muslims came as students. "She made [food] provisions for them and they did not have to eat the 'choke' sandwiches. We called them choke sandwiches because the bread was so thick as well as the salami or bologna, that we said they gave it to us to choke at night. We knew we would have an apple or orange but we went into the cafeteria and grabbed a bag not knowing what sandwich was in it. We'd barter the sandwiches. But they [Muslim students] were allowed to eat peanut butter and jelly," a respondent explained. When the climate was finally open to the school's serving both Blacks and Whites, one White student said that it didn't matter what the color was of the miscreant, Dr. Mallory took no prisoners and corporal punishment was meted out. Another White student told the story of her slapping the face of his father. And she was not punished! No small feat in the KKK infested Holmes County, Mississippi.

But Dr. Mallory learned how to walk in wisdom before those within and outside the sanctified church and school. She made friends with local businessmen. She did not allow any false pride to stand in her path when she didn't have money to pay for kerosene or other needed items. And upon receiving credit when she didn't have cash, businessmen knew she repaid her debt upon receipt of funds from her benefactors or funds were raised in Annual May Day festivities. National Supervisors Mother Annie Bailey and Mattie McGlothen were among those who sponsored the school's May Day Festivities. The Tri-State Defender "The South's Independent Weekly", boasted of

Students in formation at May Day program

serving 1,000,000 Negroes by 1952. Mallory understood the power of the press and invited a reporter to witness Saints Industrial's 12th Annual Saints Industrial May Day Parade. The May 17, 1952 headline read –

10,000 Witness May Day Festivities At Saints Industrial School Raise $4,000 to Help Erect Building

Ten thousand people thronged the streets of Lexington among both races an[d] stood from 11:00 a.m. until 2 p.m. WAITING FOR THE PARADE. The PTA, community, teachers and students under the direction of the president of the school reported more than $4,000 toward the erection of a modern day elementary school. Matching funds are expected to make a good building possible from the executive board of education of the churches of God in Christ.

The reporter stated that the crowd witnessed floats with seven foot arches and boys and girls dressed marching in costumes of various countries. The 55 piece band from the Harris High School of Meridian, MS also marched followed by the colorful float of the King and Queen and their royal court. The reporter went on to state that Holmes County provided a public address system for Dr. Mallory's use to inform the crowd of information of events on campus during the parade. This resulted in further assistance to the school from Blacks and Whites.

Speaking at National Council of Negro Women Meeting

Through Dr. Mallory's religiously based activism with organizations such as the National Council of Negro Women where her friend and mentor Mary McLeod Bethune served as founder and president, she accomplished much. She was also connected to the Alpha Kappa Alpha Sorority, the nation's oldest Greek organization. It was through this partnership that she accomplished a great feat. Because of the medical needs of Blacks in Mississippi were poor at best in 1934, Alpha Kappa Alpha sponsored the Mississippi Health Project to bring primary medical care to rural blacks. Members of the sorority financed, designed, and implemented the project, which was active for two to six weeks every summer from 1935 to 1941. The Mississippi Health Project was the brainchild of a Mississippi native and California resident, Dr. Ida Jackson. Dr. Dorothy Celeste Building Ferebee, a member of the sorority and a practicing physician in obstetrics and gynecology, was appointed the project's medical director. Initially staffed by Dr. Ferebee and volunteers, the first medical clinic was headquartered at the Saints Industrial School in Lexington, associated with the Church of God in Christ. (http://andspeakingofwhich.blogspot.com/2013/12/ida-l-jackson-and-mississippi-health.html)

FINAL THOUGHTS

Exodus 1 speaks of a spirit driving the dominant ethnic group to take steps to eliminate the perceived threat of another ethnic group. Spirits do not die. Like the midwives of the Exodus narrative, women as the conveyors of the culture, have taken steps to save. Historically, in America, there has been a real effort to minimize the accomplishments of Blacks, especially males or even in light of places like Ferguson, MO in 2015, to eliminate.

Dr. Arenia Mallory took on a seemingly impossible task as she observed the conditions of Blacks and poor people in Holmes County, Mississippi. But in her thinking if God was God and He assigned her to the task, He would provide for her and the school. Today, it seems that opposition to faith and simple morality is overwhelming. Just as Mallory, volunteers at Saints and the larger COGIC community found, a difference can be made. Like Mallory we must "pray through" to receive answers to the dilemmas facing us.

It is when we band together in seeking God and forming strategic alliances that we will do the impossible and effectuate change in our communities, our churches, our families and our land.

Excerpt from Glimpses

Dr. Arenia Conelia Mallory began her distinguished career as an assistant to a Professor James Coats (Courts) and a Miss Pinky Duncan who had started a school with grades ranging from Elementary through eighth grades. Dr. Mallory was encouraged by our Senior Bishop C.H. Mason of the Churches of God in Christ who saw the great need for a Christian Education for Black boys and girls. Bishop Mason asked Dr. Mallory to change her idea of going to Africa and go South to Lexington, Mississippi in the benighted area of Mississippi where help was needed as badly or worse than Africa. Dr. Mallory accepted his advice with the Divine guidance of God. She came to Lexington in 1926, saw the need and began to work. Not having been South before, only God could have given her the wisdom, knowledge, and understanding how to cope with the Southern customs traditions, and conditions. Shortly after Dr Mallory came to Lexington, Professor Coats died and she became head of the school.

Dr. Mallory was determined to do something to better the educational status of boys and girls in the Delta and rural sections—she called them *the forgotten children.* They did not have money nor the proper clothing. Many had no shoes, had not seen an electric light or bath tub and never had a doctor. Thousands lived on these plantations with no advantages nor encouragement toward the higher principles of life and education.

She went at night all through the plantations and talked with the parents to send their children to Saints School. They would say, we have no money, clothes or shoes to send them. Dr. Mallory would say, "Send them on." We'll give them clothes and shoes if you can spare a few potatoes, molasses, corn, anything in food for that will help us also." So some came with a gallon of syrup or some other kinds of food. The tuition for those commuting to school was only 25 cents Elementary, and 50 cents High School, and some could not pay that.

Many of her years of administration were years of toil and hardships without any visual means of supporting the school. But with faith in God, Dr. Mallory undertook the task of developing this institution. The only opportunity for financing and building the school was that of giving lectures *in Negro and White churches within America and asking for free-will contributions. Through this method of lectures and the Jubilee Harmonizers singing, the institution developed and grew.*

As it grew, the school attracted statewide attention and rapidly became nationally known. Forty or more states in the Union was represented in the student body-also Africa, West Indies and Alaska. Dr. Mallory insisted upon the old standards of morality and wholesome living. The underlying purpose of Saints Academy and Saints Jr. College in inoculating into the students the idea of scholastic competence and the ideals of true Christian character.

The year was 1931, the time America experienced the worst depression the world has ever known. June, 1931, Dr. Mallory called all the students, faculty, and staff members to join with her in prayer on the campus. Everyone got on his knees on the spot where she wanted God to give us a brick academic administration building for classes, offices, and an auditorium for we needed to get out of the prayer room. [It] was in the one building also, where prayer went on from 8 A.M. to 5 P.M. Each student took fifteen minutes during the day to stop and pray. We prayed not a long prayer but a fervent sincere prayer believing it would be done.

Inspite of the depression, Dr. Mallory said, "Children, there is no depression with God. The earth is the Lord's and the fullness there of...the cattles upon a thousand hills belong to God and He will supply our needs." At the close of the prayer, she said, "God gave me the answer. He said, New York, and Lo I am with you always even to the end of the world. Miss Lashley, get the girls ready. We are leaving as soon as I can contact Mother to see my brother Frank Mallory to drive us." She did not have to pay him. He gave his service free.

She told the contractor to start working on a brick building. He gave her the estimated cost of the building. "We'll have the money when you complete the building." We started with seven persons in a five passenger car; tank filled with gas and oil on credit. Dr. Mallory had made friends with some of the White merchants in Lexington and they trusted her to pay. We stopped along the way and sang to keep gas and oil in the car.

We ate mostly cheese and crackers and drunk soda pops. We shifted from side to side on the crowded seats, but God was with us and let us reach New York safely though tired, weary, and worn. They had a place where we all could stay together.

The next morning, we had prayer and ate cereal. Dr. Mallory called the group in the room and said, "We have no contract or know any person here who could really help us but God will open the door for us. At that time, the Methodist and Baptist people called Sanctified people fanatics and fools. They wanted no part of them. Most of our people at that time were in store fronts and were very poor. Mississippi was carrying the school at this time. She said, "I want you to get on your knees and tell God about it while Frank takes me where God directs. Stay before God until we return."

We kneeled and prayed until we heard her voice late in the afternoon. "Get up get up. Your prayers have been answered. We are booked in the largest churches in New York City for three weeks. This will make it easier to get in other churches." You could hear all over the place praising God and rejoicing. The Father of Rep. Adam Clayton Powell, Head of Education and Welfare, was the first to open his church to us. This church was one of the finest churches in New York and their membership was of the elite society.

Dr. Mallory would introduce the Harmonizers and give a few remarks as to what she was trying to do in Mississippi for the sharecroppers' children. She, then, invited them to come to the program on Monday night. She told her story and her dream and we sang. The contribution the first night was 800.00 at the Abersinia [Abyssinia] Baptist Church. People all over New York were in bread and soup lines. We saw men eating out of garbage cans. But God, the Miracle Father and the Way Maker, saw her needs and supplied them.

After eight weeks, we had raised enough money to pay in full for the brick building now recognized on Saints College campus by the name of Faith Hall. Dr. Mallory chose the name Faith Hall because, "God gave it to us by faith."

During the winter months, Dr. Mallory took the group to the state of Florida to raise the teacher's salary which would sometimes be more than a month overdue. But in those days, teachers worked and served for the love of service and love for the students rather than just the love of money. They did superb work with little grumbling or complaining. Bishop Cohen, Sr., looked forward to Dr. Mallory's coming to Florida each year. She depended on him for the balance of the teacher's salary and other current bills that money from the tour did not cover.

Dr. Mallory sacrificed and gave her life to make her dream come true. Dreams are sometimes painful and costly. She endured the pains to death's door. She paid with her all; mind, heart, soul, and body; mentally, spiritually, and physically. Through it all, she constantly admonished her children "To keep your head up, throw your shoulders back and reach for the stars. If you keep your hands in God's and, you can make it. Don't let anyone tell you can't make it. Just Walk in dignity, Talk in dignity, and Live in dignity. Be proud of your race and love God."

Chapter Three

THE LEGACY OF TWO INSTITUTIONS
Saints Junior College and Bethune-Cookman University Under Review

Willie A. Bragg

Your vision has to require a miracle to give God glory.
Presiding Bishop Charles E. Blake
Church of God in Christ, Inc.

INTRODUCTION

When one traces the life of Dr. Arenia Cornelia Mallory, words such as educator, spiritual leader, visionary, courageous, community activist come to mind that characterize her journey, her challenges, and her triumphs. Who was Dr. Mallory and what were her greatest accomplishments? Who were her advocates? Why is there so little known and written about this spiritual leader and pioneer in the educational arena? What were the educational outcomes and benefits of the relationship between Dr. Mallory and Dr. Mary McLeod Bethune? What led to the demise of Saints Junior College? As one closely examines Goodson (2016), pertinent questions emerge that surround the life and legacy of Dr. Mallory.

It is very clear that Dr. Mallory's achievements were far reaching and spread beyond Saints Junior College. Her contributions had a direct impact on many communities in Mississippi and Florida. Hence, the purpose of this essay is to highlight her accomplishments and to provide a framework to explore factors that facilitated successes of Dr. Mallory relative to the 50 years she served as president. In addition, this discussion raises critical issues about the support, culture and the implications for educational growth in the Church of God in Christ (COGIC).

EDUCATIONAL PROFILE
DR. ARENIA CONELIA MALLORY

I am a Woman
Phenomenally,
Phenomenal Woman,
That's Me

Maya Angelou, Phenomenal Woman Poem (1978)

Dr. Mallory was a well-educated, highly respected woman. She was born in 1904 in Illinois. It is interesting to note that her mother was the first African-American to master the Italian harp and singer Ethel Waters was her sister-in-law. One might suppose that her musical background was an outgrowth of strong family roots. In fact, Dr. Mallory was actually trained to be a concert pianist (Tucker, 2009). She received a Bachelor of Arts degree in 1927 from Simmons College of Kentucky, Master of Arts degree from Jackson State University (formally Jackson College) and a Master's degree in Administration from the University of Illinois at Urbana Champaign in 1950. She also received an honorary Doctor of Laws degree in 1951 from Bethune-Cookman University (formally Bethune-Cookman College) for outstanding work in Christian Education. It is not surprising to learn that many of Dr. Mallory's accomplishments paralleled the journey of Dr. Mary McLeod Bethune.

According to historical documents, they were the only two African-American female presidents in the Deep South during the early 1900s. It is the belief of the writer that Dr. Bethune may have served as a "mentor" to Dr. Mallory. It is also believed that these women shared ideas and approaches about establishing academically sound institutions grounded in religious tenets. For example, similar themes are displayed below for each institution.

Bethune-Cookman University
Enter to Learn
Depart to Serve (Flemming, 1995)

Saints Junior College
Enter to Learn
Leave to Serve (www.drmallory.org)

Key academic and religious events are outlined in the major milestones and accomplishments of Dr. Mallory.

MAJOR MILESTONES OF SAINTS SCHOOL

➢ Saints Industrial School started in basement of the St. Paul COGIC, founded by C.H. Mason, in Lexington, Mississippi
➢ Literary and Industrial School established in 1917

- Ms. Pinkie Duncan was followed by Professor Coats who served as head for eight years.
- Dr. Mallory appointed president in 1926
- Dr. Mallory served as president from 1926 – 1976
- Dr. Mallory with the help of the church developed 350 acres of land for Saints Junior College
- Saints Academy was established as "a first" school for Blacks in Mississippi
- School accredited by the State Board of Education in 1936 with addition of Saints Junior College in 1954
- Raised money for the college by speaking at African-American and white churches for free will offerings
- Raised money during COGIC Convocations with students singing and playing, lecturing, and private fundraising
- Expanded the school and academy from one building to more than 24 campus buildings with the names of COGIC women and men who provided unwavering financial support
- Names of buildings honored women (Women's Department) e.g., Mothers Bailey, Coffey, Clemmons, McGlothen, and Robinson
- Buildings honored bishops, e.g., Wells, Jones, McKinney, Washington, and Kelly

Documents confirm that Dr. Mallory was an anointed servant of God chosen to continue the dream of Saints Junior College as ordained by COGIC founder Bishop C.H. Mason. And, the environment of the school was conducive to learning. Students were involved in academic and religious training. Davis (2009), a student at Saints Junior College, shares firsthand experiences and revealing stories about life at the institution. She states the following:

At 10 o'clock, we stopped everything to have prayer. The hall monitor that week would start singing. *Whisper a prayer in the morning. Whisper a prayer at no-oo-oo-on.* The rest of us would join in as we all congregated downstairs and knelt on the floor in front of chairs and couches. We went through prayer ritual (p. 214).

Davis (2009) further shares reflections about singing and praying at the annual COGIC meetings in Memphis, Tennessee: Dr. Mallory hand-picked people from the glee club, choir, and band to travel to Memphis. (p. 219)

When time came for us to perform, we went to our assigned areas to march in. Saints' entrances were something to see. We were the *joint*. The band marched first. We were marching in from three different entrances, bringing our knees up to our chests as we moved down four aisles moving towards the stage where our stands were set up. We swung our instruments from side to side moving to the drums rhythmic beat. We stopped swinging our instruments on cue from the Major Domo, and began to play. When we were all in place on stage, we ended the music, and sharply pulled our instruments down to our side in sync. The audience roared and clapped their approval...(p.221-222). The choir marched in singing. They were swinging from side to side, every voice in perfect harmony. Everyone was confidently smiling. It was a sight to see.

Davis (2009) also reports in her writing the vision of Dr. Mallory:

Her Vision - Our Mission

Dr. Mallory's vision and goal was to provide an education, instill pride, confidence, and self-sufficiency in every individual and family within Holmes County and beyond. She also provided spiritual guidance in order to instill faith and belief in God within everyone with whom she came into contact.

Her life was and is a living testimony of her strong faith in God and her Christ-like dealings with others. No person who was hungry, without clothing, shelter, needed medical attention, or lacking an education was turned away, or denied help if they came to her, or she heard of their plight. She ALWAYS found a way, or ways to make room for them, or assigned someone to them, or their families to assure their needs were taken care of until they could become self-sufficient, productive citizens without the yoke of poverty weighing them down.

EDUCATIONAL PROFILE
DR. MARY MCLEOD BETHUNE:

(Pictured above, Dr. Bethune holds the cane of President Theodore Roosevelt)

Dr. Bethune, born in South Carolina in 1875 was an educator and civil rights activist. She received her preparation at Moody Bible Institute (formally Bible Institute for Home and Foreign Missions) in Chicago. She completed the program in two years and won a scholarship to attend Barber Scotia College (formally Scotia Seminary). Dr. Bethune, similar to Dr. Mallory, believed that education was the way to racial opportunity (Podesta, 2016). Dr. Bethune and Dr. Mallory stressed religious values and faith in God as the essential foundation of their respective institutions. Realizing the importance of accreditation, these African-American pioneers confronted many obstacles in the quest to establish accredited educational institutions. They knew that accreditation was a type of endorsement that the college or university had valid programs that were recognized by the U.S. Department of Education. Furthermore, it would verify that the institution of higher education met the acceptable level of quality. One can imagine how difficult it must have been to obtain accreditation during the years Drs. Mallory and Bethune served as presidents. Comparison of major milestones illustrates the tremendous growth of each institution.

MAJOR MILESTONES OF BETHUNE-COOKMAN UNIVERSITY

Close examination of the birth of Bethune-Cookman University shows similar patterns of development under the leadership of Dr. Mary McLeod Bethune. Her education, faith in God, political savvy, and determination were directed toward starting a school that would advance educational opportunities for African-American students as seen in Dr. Bethune's "dream unfolded in Daytona" (Flemming, 1995). The following events chronicle her accomplishments relative to establishing Bethune-Cookman University:

- ➢ Dr. Bethune was born in 1875 and arrived in Daytona Beach, Florida in 1904
- ➢ Served as president for 20 years, from 1923 – 1943
- ➢ Started the school with $1.50 and five little girls and rented a four-room cottage
- ➢ Opened the door of the Daytona Literary and Industrial School for training Negro girls (DLIS) , October 4, 1904

- Names of the five little girls: Lena, Lucille, and Ruth Warren, Anna Geiger, Celeste Jackson
- Construction of the first building, Faith Hall in 1907 and increased enrollment to 250 students
- Raised money for the school from donations and community contributions
- Performance of choir at hotels, homes, and at public events raised money for the school
- Established first new hospital adjacent to school in 1911
- The DLIS increased enrollment to 30 girls, 25 faculty and staff and eight buildings in 1923
- Transferred school into college with the major goal of preparing teachers in 1923
- Official merger of Cookman Institute for men and Daytona Normal and Industrial School for girls and gained United Methodist affiliation in 1925
- Merger doubled enrollment to approximately 600 students and became Bethune-Cookman College in 1929
- Institution received accreditation from the Southern Association of Colleges and Schools (SACS) in 1931
- Officially changed name to Bethune-Cookman College in 1931
- Graduated students from a four-year teacher education program in 1943

Given Dr. Bethune's leadership qualities, business savvy, political acumen and belief in God, she was extremely effective in galvanizing support (e.g., philanthropists, businessmen, presidents) to promote the institution as well as addressing social concerns. From the vantage point of the writer, Drs. Bethune and Mallory may be considered today **the voices of social justice.**

COMMUNITY/SOCIAL ACTIVISM OF TWO PRESIDENTS

Drs. Mallory and Bethune addressed social and environmental conditions impacting rural areas. Upon Dr. Bethune's arrival in Daytona Beach, Florida, she found "meager education facilities and social prejudice" (Flemming, 1995). Similarly, Dr. Mallory viewed Saints Junior College as the point of centrality for social issues and solutions. According to Goodson's review (2016), Dr. Mallory was a lady of *firsts*. She established the first campus health program in the community (Holmes County). She initiated the first adult education classes and was instrumental in initiating the first county migrant farm adult education program on the campus in 1966. Her influence in healthcare can be seen in current Dr. Arenia C. Mallory community health centers serving over 50 communities in areas including Durant and Lexington, Mississippi. It is interesting to note the motto of health centers: *Enter a patient, leave a friend.*

One can also observe the lasting influence in the community while driving on the street named in her honor. Recognizing the importance of early education for African-American children and parents, Dr. Mallory established the first Head Start program in 1965. She was consultant for the U.S. Department of Labor in 1963. She was the first woman, and first African-American woman, elected to the Holmes County Board of Education.

Dr. Bethune also devoted considerable time to social/community and political issues (Flemming, 1995; Podesta, 2016). Under President Coolidge, Dr. Bethune was involved in a child-welfare conference. During President

Hoover's administration, she was a member of the Child Health Committee. Perhaps one of her most nationally recognized appointments was that of national advisor to President Roosevelt on minority affairs. Furthermore, Dr. Bethune worked closely with First Lady Eleanor Roosevelt as did Dr. Mallory as a member of Mrs. Roosevelt's Negro Women's League, a group that advised her on African-American issues from a woman's perspective. Frequently, Drs. Bethune and Mallory would travel to the White House to discuss issues regarding education, health, and welfare of individuals living in economically disadvantaged rural communities. Dr. Bethune served as a New Deal government official—one of the 20 highest positions held by a woman, particularly an African-American woman.

Drs. Bethune and Mallory were advocates of gender equity and the advancement of African-American women. Dr. Bethune served as president of the National Association of Colored Women (NACW) and she was founder of the National Council of Negro Women (NCNW). She served as president of NCNW from 1939 – 1949. Dr. Mallory served as Vice President from 1953 – 1957. Both women were committed to the women's rights movement during this time. It is the opinion of the writer that Drs. Bethune and Mallory believed African-American women, in particular, must be equipped to "lead" and therefore must be well grounded spiritually, educationally, and professionally.

CLOSING THOUGHTS: TWO LEADERS, TWO LEGENDS, TWO OUTCOMES

This essay presents the lives and legacies of two African-American pioneers who were visionaries and social change agents. It also explores the creation of two institutions of higher education highlighting significant events that facilitated the expansion of the institutions. What is evident and perhaps the underlying success of these institutions is that they were established with a strong spiritual foundation. It further presents major benchmarks during the developmental phases of each university. Through comparisons of educational institutions, Drs. Bethune and Mallory saw the need to be involved in community welfare and social justice reform. It is also clear that they were highly anointed, spirit-filled, dedicated leaders. Dr. Mallory served as president for 50 years and Dr. Bethune established and remained as president for 20 years. They both were extremely successful in obtaining support from philanthropists, businessmen, community representatives, political and government allies, and religious groups. Considering the support and similarities relative to approaches and strategies to development and grow the institutions, one would anticipate similar outcomes.

Today, Bethune-Cookman University offers an array of undergraduate, graduate, and online programs to more than 3,500 students. The university maintains its SACS accreditation along with specific accreditations for individual schools and colleges. The Mary McLeod Bethune Home is a historical monument on campus which marks the legacy of her contributions. White Hall has been added to the National Register of Historic Places. On a professional note, the writer of this essay served as a faculty member and director of the School of Education's Teacher Education Institute. She has firsthand experiences working with outstanding faculty and students from culturally and linguistically diverse backgrounds. Several buildings with signage along with campus and community events reflect Dr. Bethune's *answered prayer to a dream.*

Saints Junior College also has a rich history. It is estimated that over 25,000 students attended the institution. It is instructive to note that COGIC leaders including Bishops L.H. Ford attended this fine institution. Additionally, class reunions celebrate the contributions of Dr. Mallory. She had a remarkable influence on students who attended Saints Junior College. Davis (2009) shares her views:

"I wouldn't trade my experiences at Saints for anything. It enriched my life in many ways. Plus, I have a unique group of friends from all over the country and Africa"...I have crossed many bridges in my life. Looking back now I know Saints Junior College was a vital piece of the puzzle in my life that had to exist in order for me to become who I am. Without it, I would not be as proud of myself as a black woman, or as proud of my people, and our collective Diaspora in this country.

It was at Saints that I subconsciously began my research about black history. It was there, that the fire that still burns in my soul for equality and justice was first ignited...I left Saints with a strong conviction that we all have a vested interest in seeing all of our people grow in high self-esteem, pride, commitment to excellence, economic freedom and service to each other...Dr. Mallory exposed us to so much during our stay at Saints...She did not allow us to depart Mississippi without exposing us to the towns so that we could see for ourselves the condition of our people and the work that needed to be done to improve those conditions" (p.228).

Saints Academy, i.e., school, also had tremendous effects on students. During a recent interview with a former Saints Academy student (personal communication, March, 2016), he gave a vivid account of his time at Saints Academy in 1969. He recalled how structured the school was and how students moved from class to class in straight lines, somewhat in a marching style. All students attended church services two evenings each week and participated in daily Bible study classes. He reflected on his activities, including the trip to the Holy Convocation in Memphis, Tennessee—a required trip. It was one of the few times he actually saw Dr. Mallory because she seemed to be very busy raising money for the school.

He further recalled that the curriculum had a very strong religious focus which he felt provided a good atmosphere for learning. Similar to his enrollment status, other students at Saints Academy were children of parents who were members of COGIC. During the interview he mentioned that students from the surrounding communities also attended the school. In some cases, students who attended Saints Academy had experienced as he termed, "problems in the public school." At Saints Academy, everything was provided for the students. When posed the question, What were the advantages and disadvantages of attending Saints Academy, he responded, "there were no disadvantages, but the advantage was, it was a good, well-structured school." When asked the final question that related to the existence of the school, the former student felt that it would be a good school for today, but thought the program changes would center around the use of the Internet.

Where are we today with Saints Junior College? According to COGIC records, Saints Junior College closed in 1983. What happened to a thriving institution that Bishop Mason envisioned as vital to the growth and history of COGIC? Hall (1990) provides a crucial account of events that occurred during a Saints Center Board meeting about Saints Junior College. According to Hall's editorial comments in The *Whole Truth* in 1990, Bishop Ford "issued the challenge to saints for the immediate reopening of Saints Academy." Hall further notes that the only obstacle in the way of the goal was the Multi-Service Building. Hall's editorial seems to suggest that this building was to be constructed upon a hill on the center of Saints Junior College. As a result, the Saints Center resolution was developed at that board meeting stating the following: "Now therefore, be it resolved that we thereby pledge the funds to the leadership of the church. Be it further resolved that we thereby pledge the funds to construct the J.O. Patterson and Deborah Mason Patterson Multi-Purpose Dining Hall in Lexington, Mississippi." Hall (1990) comments that "when Bishop Ford reopens the Saints Academy in Lexington, Mississippi, there will be a new sparkle in the jewel of the campus."

Based on this account, one would believe that the outcome for Saints Junior College was fully supported by the church. The pledge to provide funds to construct a new building appeared to signal a renewed commitment to reopen the college, an accredited institution. One would also believe that a decision relative to the only educational unit and dream of the COGIC founder would have the full support and involvement of the church leadership at all levels. How did Bethune-Cookman University continue to expand as a well-established thriving institution of higher education while Saints Junior College and Academy became the forgotten institution that ceased to exist?

It is clear that the educational and economic climate during the 1950s affected the expansion and "staying power" of Saints Junior College. According to Tucker (2009), competing forces from public and private institutions to attract high achieving African-American students to their institutions contributed to the closing of Saints. Dwindling resources coupled with limited administrative and financial support of COGIC made it difficult for the religious-based Saints Junior College and Academy to maintain its resilience, relevance and academic rigor and appeal to a broader e.g., (Methodist, International) student body.

Fast forward to the present educational landscape, one may view similarities of the plight of Saints to current challenges facing Historically Black Colleges and Universities (HBCUs). There is a plethora of literature addressing the struggles of small and private HBCUs relative to funding, academic programs, enrollment, and resources (Anderson, 2016; Carter, 2016; Gardner, 2016; Lynch, 2013; and Wright, 2016). Private and State institutions, including Predominantly White Institutions (PWIs) aggressively pursue the "best and brightest" students of color e.g., African-Americans. Such well-endowed institutions offer lucrative financial packages, scholarships, and early mentoring benefits to attract students to the university. New and tenured faculty of color are also recruited to PWIs with offers of abundant resources, research incentives, reduced teaching loads, and opportunities for career advancements. As these institutions increase student enrollment and faculty under the broad umbrella of diversity, small HBCUs show signs of decreased student population and faculty pool along with dwindling resources and financial support. The closing of some small and private HBCUs is becoming more frequently reported in the educational community and mirrors similar circumstances surrounding the closing of Saints.

What are the lessons learned from the past, that is, Saints Junior College and the present HBCUs that will serve as the blueprint for sustainability? Case in point: the Interdenominational Theological Center (ITC), a consortium of six Christian seminaries, including C.H. Mason Seminary, plays a significant role in COGIC history today. ITC is a unique collaboration, accredited by SACS and holds accreditation in the Association of Theological Schools (ATS) in the United States and Canada. According to the ITC website,

C.H. Mason Seminary is viewed as one of the few accredited African-American Pentecostal seminaries in the U.S. offering Master's and Doctoral degree programs. Furthermore, it is seen as one of the few academic units administratively governed and financially support by COGIC.

Given the current landscape in higher education, it is the opinion of this writer that for religious-based institutions to survive, the focus must be completely embraced by the administrative arm of COGIC. The institution must also utilize best practices. As evidenced at Bethune-Cookman University during Dr. Mary McLeod Bethune's presidency, the institution must also be financially sound, curriculum relevant, with faculty trained to prepare students in a religious environment. For an institution to survive and expand nationally, as Dr. Mallory attempted to do as Saints Junior College, the program must be academically strong with cutting-edge research opportunities that promote the religious goals of the institution. Finally, the institution must have a well-established senior leadership committed to, and accountable for supporting the vision of the founder, Bishop Charles Harrison Mason. These components are vital to the existence of strong institutions. As such, they are key elements necessary to the growth and sustainability of COGIC's **only** accredited seminary. It is hoped that the vision and purpose of the founder (Mason) will not be lost but will exemplify his spirit through life-long learning at C.H. Mason Seminary in the 21st Century and beyond.

Excerpt from Glimpses

The Bible says the Roots of the Righteous shall never be moved. Some of the thousands Dr. Mallory touched who reached the stars have attended colleges all over the United States. These are the Roots of Saints Jr. College and Academy, and are Dr. Mallory's contribution to the community, the state, the nation, and the world. Children who will make the world a better place in which to live. They were taught education alone will not suffice. They must keep their lives in tune with God. Without help from the Master Tuner, their lives would be filled with discard and confusion.

[Miss] Duncan passed and Professor James Coats became the Head of the school…two frame buildings on stilts with roughly made seats without any sanitary facilities no lights outside, hand pump for water, kerosene oil lamps, water heated in a large iron pot outside for baths, tin tub and wash board for laundry, wood stove heater, and wood for heating the buildings and for kitchen use was cut in the woods by the young men. Education all over Holmes County was limited to eight grades.

The first payment on the present site, then, a large plantation was paid by the members of the Mississippi Churches of God in Christ and friends.

Under Dr. Mallory's Administration over a period of 50 years, she has developed a portion of the 350 acres of land into a beautiful attractive campus with shrubbery and trees planted, paved roads, and paved sidewalks and lights outside and inside all buildings. The college is sitting along side of Highway 17 sixty miles north of Mississippi's capital city, Jackson, Mississippi. As you reach the top of the hill and see the lights on Saints College campus, you might be lead to believe that you are approaching the Town of Lexington. In the beginning, there was no lights but God said let there be lights and there was lights.

In 1936, Saints Industrial and Literary School (known today as Saints Academy) had the distinction of being one of the first schools for Negro students in Mississippi to be fully accredited by the State Department of Education. Also, the first high school for Black children in the entire county organized. The first health Program for the black community was sponsored on Saints campus by the Alpha Kappa Alpha National Sorority. The first adult education classes in the country were held on campus and taught by teacher volunteers.

In 1966, Saints campus was the site for the Migrant Farm Adult Education Program, Second Start (first in the county) Sponsored by the Office of Economic Opportunity in Washington, D.C. This program opened opportunities for the poorest families in the poorest counties to have basic education and other opportunities in skills.

In 1965, the first Head Start classes in this area was funded by OEC on Saints Campus. September 1977 began the 12th Program for these deprived children.

Under the Administration of President Mallory, she added 4 grades and Saints Industrial School became the first High school for Negroes in Holmes County and was accredited by the State of Mississippi Accrediting Commission with an A. A. rating. The Two-year College was added 1957. The College and Academy have grown [to] living quarters for faculty, students, kitchen, dining room, offices, classroom upstairs for Elementary grades; wood stove, water for bath heated outside from a large iron pot; no modern conveniences.

Today we have 16 Major Buildings: Faith Hall, President's Office, Mason-Coffey Building with B.S. Lyles Auditorium and Alumni Library, Industrial Arts Building, Mechanical Arts Building, 10 brick buildings, 6 frame buildings, 6 Trailer Buildings used for housing faculty and staff, Offices, etc. All total from 1 building to 22 buildings. Saints Junior College and Saints Academy is now valued at approximately one million dollars ($1,000,000.00). Buildings on the campus includes a modern college administration building with modern science rooms, class rooms, modern Alumni Library, Faith Hall, The High School Administration Building with classrooms, Principal's Office, Business Office, Financial Aid Office and Wyoming Wells Auditorium with the capacity of 1,000. The Andrea M. Clemmons Children Center.

The Sargent Shriver Children Clinic and Dining Hall, built by the Migrant Farm Education Project under OEO. Sargent Shriver was Director of OEO., Washington, D.C. at this time.

Gamble Rice Hall, Boy's High School Dormitory, erected and paid for under the leadership of Bishop B.S. Lyles-the tenth year as President of the Board of Directors.

Jones Hall Girl's High School Dormitory, a gift from the National Youth Congress of the Churches of God in Christ under the Administration of Bishop O.T. Jones, Sr., President and Supervisor Hearn of Okla.

Alexander Houston Industrial Arts Building, Bishop J.E. Alexander and Supervisor Houston, Midland, Texas.

Mechanical Arts Industrial Building, erected by President Mallory through the Federal Government OEO. Mallory Hall, modern Elementary building. One room a gift from the Women's Department of the Church of God in Christ under the Administration of Mother Lillian Brooks Coffey. Five other rooms, concrete porch, two modern rest rooms gifts from the P.T.A. of Saints Jr. College High, President, Staff, and Student body through the May Day Drive.

Lizzy Robinson Dining Hall, a $75,000 modern refectory, a gift from the Women's Department of the Church of God in Christ under the supervision of Mother Lillian Brooks Coffey. The Peyton House, a gift from the Women's Dept. of the Church of God in Christ under the Administration of Mother M. Peyton, Supervisor. Snack bar, gift from Bishop Carr of Baltimore, Maryland — All the inside furnishing, electrical equipped kitchen, one added room with modern leather booths and tables, and extra side walk enhance over three thousand dollars — Supervisor, E.M. Lashley.

The Annie L. Bailey College residence Hall for young women, modern two story building dedicated 1972. This building was made possible under the Federal Housing Act with the assistan[ce] of the Government. The beautiful lounge was furnished by Bishop and Mrs. Dell, Atlanta, Ga. Each room was furnished by the donor whose name appears over the door.

The McGlothen Guest House, given by Mother Mattie McGlothen. She is now the National Supervisor of Women of the Church of God in Christ–Richmond, Ca.

Frederick Douglas Washington Residence Hall for College men, two story modern brick building dedicated 1972. This building was made possible under the Federal Housing Act with the assistan[ce] of the Government. Each room was furnished by the donor whose name appears over the door.

O.M. Kelly Chapel, gift from Bishop and Mrs. O.M. Kelly – carpet by Mrs. Maude Kelly – Podium gift from Evangelist Willis.

Hammond organ by Bishop and Mrs. Leroy Anderson.

Gold Cross for O.M. Kelly Chapel by Dr. Dorothy S. Ferbee, Washington, D.C.

Kivie Kaplin, Shelves of valuable books, Boston, Mass.

Two school buses, gift from Saints College and Snack Bar.

Draperies, dishes, silver, kitchen utensils, gift from Supervisor, J.V. Hearn. Refrigerator for the refectory, gift from Bishop J.S. Bailey.

Piano for B.S. Lyles Auditorium, Bishop D. Burton.

Chimes (worth over $3,000.00) music from the chimes can be heard all over the town of Lexington, by Mother Jessie Washington.

Mother Fannie Beck made Dr. Mallory Executor of her Will before she (Mother Beck) died and in that Will a gift of $25,000.00 was left to Saints College and Academy.

Dr. Malory added six Trailer Houses to the Campus during her Administration. One double wide trailer specially made for College Dining

One double wide trailer used for the President's Office and house the trophies, awards, etc. of President Mallory. The other four trailers were used for faculty members housing.

Dr. Mallory, also, had worked on a plan to build a gymnasium for the students. The Blue Print was drawn up and bids had been taken for the contract to build it. One gentleman had offered to give $25,000.00 toward this building.

Bishop W.L. McKenny gave the first water fountain to the school. It yet stands in Jones Hall. He gave it in honor of his daughter Evangelist McKenny Beaudoir, Los Angeles, Calif.

Chapter Four

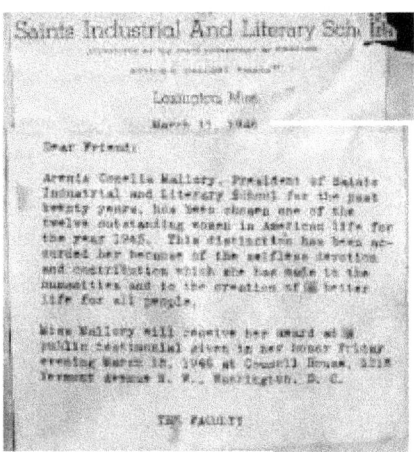

Arenia C. Mallory's Leadership Revisited:
Perspectives on Education, Politics, Culture and Community

Cynthia Barbara Bragg

There is a great responsibility laid on those whom God has made choice of. Let us seek God for wisdom, that we may know how, when and what to do...that we may be able to approve things that are excellent. Mother Annie Bailey

INTRODUCTION

The following is an excerpt from the 1946(?) *Whole Truth* concerning Dr. Mallory's work with the Lexington, Mississippi: school

President Mallory has established a school that will live for generations to come. There should be a building erected on this campus and dedicated to this great woman. President Arenia C. Mallory, who has pave[d] the way in the heat of the day edu[ca]ting the youth for the leadership in a new day.

To know President Mallory you must come in contact with her and then you will find a brilliant leader with an humble and very meek spirit. Her lovely personality with magnetic power that [is]? a significant influence to always gain new friends. You will never know or realize the value of President Mallory until you visit this school.

Mallory's dream of going as a missionary to Africa changed once she recognized that her calling would be "Little Africa" in Lexington, Mississippi. Little did she know at the time that she was destined to become a woman of great influence, a mentor, and a teacher to many the Lord would bless her to meet.

Dr. Arenia C. Mallory was an educator, a leader, and an activist. Her lifelong commitment of building an institution linked her community "uplift" efforts of the 1920s and 1930s to broader struggles for educational equality and economic justice during the early years of presidency at Saints Junior College. Cultural programs that she was a part of and the institution (Saints Junior College) she served were key to her articulation of Black community consciousness in reference to the Church Of God In Christ (COGIC) and community at large. She formed a coalition with churchwomen and civic leaders drawing attention to the long struggle for educational opportunities for African-Americans. Her efforts were part of a broader tradition of black churchwomen's agency that contributed to ongoing community-building efforts central to the Black church generally and COGIC in particular. Mallory's community engagement formed a "cultural base" of sustainability with leaders thus enabling her to keep the focus on equitable education, economic advancement, political representation and social parity. Ultimately, Mallory's involvements would become part of a broader social network expanding both nationally and internationally.

Dr. Mallory grew up in Jacksonville, Illinois and began her career spanning 50 years in Lexington, Mississippi. During the earlier years of her life, her aspirations were to become a concert pianist performing on stages around the world to entertain people. After receiving the Baptism of the Holy Ghost at age 17, she came to the realization that her missionary "call" in life was to go to Lexington, Mississippi. According to Lovett (2003), the request of Bishop Charles Harrison Mason who was led to assign Mallory to head Saints Industrial and Literary School in Lexington, Mississippi was accepted by her. Simmons and Martin (1983:114) record an article by Mallory in *The Durant News* in 1976. She reminisces about her life's journey while thanking the citizens and friends of Mississippi and Holmes County for their unwavering support. In this correspondence she states:

I wanted to be a welfare worker or an educator in Liberia, Africa; [Mason] inspired me to come here. I found my life's work in a cotton field; two frame buildings that were not modernized, and the only light you could see at night was the Court House dome. Not a green tree...A small pump furnished our water and an iron pot heated it when needed.

Today, Saints has a beautiful campus, modern buildings and a good staff. We are being evaluated for Southern Association Accreditation. If we succeed, it will be our crowning achievement.

You are responsible for much of our progress; the merchants by their faith in our future, friends who never said "no" when we needed them: As I retire from the Presidency—I OWE YOU SO MUCH: Please cooperate with the new President and help Saints to continue to grow; then my service (and service of others) these fifty years will not be in vain.

DEVELOPING YEARS

When Mallory was first appointed as president of the college, she had envisioned staying for only a short period of time. The journey she now embarked upon would be one of great sacrifice and dedication to a school and students she would love and serve with the help of God.

Dr. Mallory became a lifetime member of the Church Of God In Christ. The pioneering work of Anjulet Tucker's (2009) dissertation entitled *"Get the Learnin' but don't lose the Burnin'"; The Socio-Cultural and Religious Politics of Education in a Black Pentecostal College"* chronicles the life of Mallory and the rise and fall of an educational institution owned and operated by the Church Of God In Christ. She presents clear evidence of Mother Lillian B. Coffey's collaborative efforts with Dr. Mallory to support educational advancement at Saints Junior College. Tucker points out that Coffey's suggestion of having "the National Church [dedicate] Children's day of its annual National Convocation to raising money exclusively for the educational divisions of the church" (p. 70) should be instituted. This, Coffey believed, would eliminate frequent calls for money for educational purposes during General Assembly meetings and would be a better arrangement for all concerned.

While Mason governed the church during his lifetime, Mallory's work involving the formative years of the school's development was not constrained by "typical bureaucratic structures" associated with COGIC rules or authority. (Goodson 2015:88) gives a candid account of Mason's support of women in her essay, *The Church of God in Christ Transforms Women's Ministries Through the Positive Influence of Chief Apostle*

Bishop C.H. Mason. Mason's consistent support of the women is noted when Mallory is quoted as saying, "He demanded that men and women give me a chance to build an institution for the church that he gave his life for. He sent his own children when we didn't have an electric light, nothing but mud. He visited several times a year." Goodson asserts that "in his active years he attended every board meeting."

Efforts, however, for Mallory to maintain support for resources and teachers constantly posed new and other ways of bringing in money to the school. Not surprisingly, large amounts of funds came from the Women's Department to aid in supporting teachers and the youth attending the school. With the support of Mason, Mothers Coffey, Bailey, McGlothen and the entire Women's Department, $75,000 helped to furnish the Dining Hall at Saints (Goodson: 88). Mallory was also able to establish formal networks and relationships with prominent individuals in communities, churches, local, state, and national levels to raise funds for the school. In a taped recording, Supervisor Mother Mattie McGlothen presents evidence of the women's continual financial support to education, the church and its ministries. She states:

Let's go together...let's go back to tell you some things the women have accomplished...almost three fourths of the church today are women—we are 90% churchwomen...God has blessed the women and their pocketbooks are not empty...Since 1975, we have done a few things...We (women) went to Haiti and built a home for the senior citizens and unwed mothers...In 1985, we purchased the McGlothen House—a home for the retired mothers of the church. In 1986, we passed the Deborah Mason Patterson Scholarship Foundation for students. We have contributed thousands of dollars from the Women's Department (Bragg:1992).

Dr. Mallory was also quite ingenious in approaches to keep money

money coming to the school over the years. It was not uncommon for her to take a singing group of students from the school and sing to people in the cotton fields (who gave nickels and dimes as a donation) or stop by little churches on her way to a large city asking for a time to speak to the people. Lovett (2003) points out that Dr. Mallory organized a singing group called the Harmonizers who traveled the U.S. to solicit money for the school. On one occasion, she took a singing group to New York from the school to perform in churches in order to get donations in support of the school. Leaving Mississippi with meager funds, by faith they traveled to New York and ended up singing in the largest Protestant church in New York at that time—Abyssinian Baptist Church. As a memory of this trip, Faith Hall was erected on the campus to commemorate this trip as a faith journey. Faith Hall was the first brick building that was supported by the late Reverend Adam Clayton Powell, Abyssinian Baptist Church in New York City, making possible the erecting of this building during the Depression of 1930 (Simmons & Martin 1983:102).

Faith Hall on the campus of Saints Junior College
Source: www.dracmallory.org

CHURCH OF GOD IN CHRIST PRESIDING BISHOP L.H.FORD: PIONEER WOMEN OF THE CHURCH

Bishop Louis Henry Ford was a graduate of Saints Junior College who later became the Presiding Bishop of the Church

Of God In Christ, Incorporated following the death of Bishop James Oglethorpe Patterson, Sr. Characteristically, Ford was a charismatic and energetic leader of the church. Calvin L. Burns reports in the *Tri-State Defender Newspaper*, November 1990 that the first 8-day national Holy Convocation was held in Memphis, Tennessee—the national headquarters site of the COGIC. With more than 40,000 people expected to attend, Bishop Ford admonished the "saints to [return to] the old landmark." Ford commented that "this year's convocation theme is 'Roots: Rediscovering Our Church of God in Christ Heritage'."

This "new" Presiding Bishop undoubtedly had memories of his experiences at Saints Junior College under the tutelage of Arenia Mallory and her impact on the culture and the people. Notice of scarce references to churchwomen in leadership positions subsequently minimizing their voice and visibility is, unobtrusively expressed in a correspondence sent to officials of the church in 1991 from Presiding Bishop L. H. Ford. In the letter, Ford states that the Deborah Mason Patterson/Arenia Mallory Memorial Multi- Purpose Hall would soon be under construction in Lexington, named in honor of these women. He pointed out that Deborah Mason Patterson was the daughter of founder Charles Mason and Arenia Mallory had been president of COGIC's institution of learning for many years…Among its features, Ford stated, will be the Mallory Library containing artifacts of the late Deborah Mason Patterson, our Sainted Founder, C. H. Mason, church pioneers, executive housing, offices, conference rooms and two (2) dining halls seating 500 persons in one and 200 in the other. The plans for this project, which will be an excellent site for retreats, conferences and recreation, are 98% complete. This act by Ford was an effort to elevate the status and value of

Deborah Mason Patterson/Arenia Mallory Multi-Purpose Building

women and memorialize their names in honor of work done in the church.

The *Holmes County Herald* (1992) reports that "COGIC Leadership Raises Steeple Goals," by putting the steeple in place on the Multi-Purpose Building on the Campus of Saints Junior College. "Ford sentimentally recalled days long ago as a student,"…He shared the vision with Mallory concerning a building where people could go and pray…where people could be trained …he envisioned apartment buildings and a resort… [Ford] also wanted to erect statues of Mason and Mallory on the hillside near the Multi-Purpose facility."

SOME COMMUNITY ENDEAVORS OF DR. MALLORY

The Great Depression had a devastating effect on Black communities. The scarcity of money to support community initiatives and dwindling social outreach activities sponsored by

Black churches were negatively impacted. In many cases, however, some Black churches managed to be involved in urban politics which provided a platform for mobilizing the Black vote in larger cities. Consequently, this became part of the political machine against further devastation of Black communities economically, socially, and politically. Tensions between Black churches in particular to not take a depoliticized position was a major concern. Politically, depoliticized churches would eliminate the continued space needed to mobilize Black voters and provide a forum where political candidates could address members of Black communities. The Lincoln and Mamiya study (1990:120) points out that even during this time, "black pastors like Martin Luther King, Sr., led members of Ebenezer Baptist Church in an attempt to register to vote in 1935 in Atlanta."

Black churchwomen noted the urgency of the situation and supported their communities by leading the women's conventions of their denominations. Several high profile women such as Mary McLeod Bethune, Nannie Helen Burroughs, and Arenia Mallory were active in the national political scene as well as in the women's conventions of their denominations. Of special note, both Mallory and Mother Lillian Brooks-Coffey had close ties with Bethune as partners in the political environment as well as in ministries and educational endeavors.

During this period in history, Dr. Mallory may be viewed as an individual involved in the "cultural climate of church politics" while continuing to be an advocate for educational opportunities for Black youth and racial justice. Not only did she emphasize the need for political and social justice, Mallory's philosophy concerning life was also centered on gender justice and equality for everyone regardless of race or color. She was not deterred from her mission in life when confronted by the Ku Klux Klan concerning her welcoming White instructors at the school to work as volunteers. Mallory's purpose and anointed call in life coupled with her deep and abiding faith enabled her to ignore the racial and discriminatory threats imposed by the Klan. Mallory did, however, encourage the female volunteers to return to California. Ultimately, however, justice did prevail! On the campus where she was threatened with lynching because three White young ladies came from California to teach, during the 60s, people from all nations were employed—Blacks, Whites, Yellows, and Reds. Simmons & Martin (1983:33)) report that they were all working together as one "big family!"

POLITICAL INVOLVEMENT

Dr. Mallory was a member of the Academy of Political Science founded in 1880 by Columbia University and was later incorporated in New York State as a non-profit organization with open membership to all who paid dues. The website of this organization more recently listed information concerning the academy's sponsored conferences with organizations and institutions that deal with social issues such as homelessness, community service, and education. Of particular interest to this writer, is one of the academy's three-fold educational mission statements noted: "To educate members of the general public so they become better informed participants in the democratic process." Therefore, it seems reasonable to assume that one of Mallory's objectives for being a member of the organization was to aid in educating people politically in order to be a more informed voter, gain knowledge about public figures and community service, explore the process of governing and public policies. Having access to firsthand knowledge and information at this level could have been beneficial to churches and community leaders in helping to bring about social and political change by voting and lobbying when and where it was deemed necessary.

Dr. Mallory also had involvement with the U.S. government. She served as Manpower Specialist and Consultant for the U.S. Department of Labor during the Kennedy administration (Lovett 2003:860). Kennedy's Manpower Development and Training Act (MDTA) of 1962 focused on addressing large scale unemployment during a recession. Among other areas of concern were labor relations, wages, unemployment insurance, health plans and benefits, income, training, hiring, and economic development, to name a few. Goodson (2016) points out that Mallory's assignment as consultant involved minority group problems relative to unemployment.

Additionally, the development of college based regional centers for the MDTA focusing on training in rural areas would have been of particular interest to Mallory. The Depression had substantially weakened the U.S. economic system leaving individuals and families economically unstable. Uncertainties about their future in terms of economic survival were of major concern. The mission of the MDTA was to train and retrain unemployed workers who needed new skills and training to make adjustments to a different world of automation and technological change. As such, any governmental assistance or plan for some imperatives/initiatives was welcomed by Mallory. Since she also had inside connections to the White House, this placed her in a key position to continue as an advocate for her people.

DR ARENIA MALLORY IN HOLMES COUNTY AND LEXINGTON, MISSISSIPPI

There are several civic, community, and educational involvements that may be viewed as community programs initiated by Mallory. Seeing the great need for educational advancement as well as community uplift, she endeavoured to meet the many needs of people in Holmes County and Lexington, Mississippi in particular. Reported in the *Holmes County Herald* are programs that exemplify Mallory's efforts that helped to sustain Saints Junior College during her tenure as president. The December 1, 1966 *Holmes County Herald* newspaper reports that Saints Junior College received funding from HUD to finance two new dormitories. The school was also awarded $33,939 (for six months) to establish a Head Start program for 60 preschool children. At that time, areas classified as having extreme poverty were eligible for 100% support from local and national governments. In conjunction with the Head Start program at Saints which was funded the previous summer, there was an elementary and high school component. The program aided the children of tenant farmers who attended classes three months a year. During that era, it served as the *only* high school for Black students in the county. Dr. Mallory served as staff director over six professionals, with eight resident employees managing program activities. These federal grants were all to support development and expansion in Holmes County and the surrounding areas.

The September 1966 *Holmes County Herald* newspaper also reported there were 120 students that graduated from a homemaker training program (12 weeks) sponsored by the Mississippi Department of Public Welfare. This program provided practical training related to modern homemaking and adult education courses. Training was designed to foster self-empowerment and vocational specialization enabling individuals to become more employable. As such, the former domestic worker developed skills necessary to compete for jobs in restaurants, hotels, and the motel industries. Basic courses also focused on reading, writing, and arithmetic. The courses were administered through Saints Junior College facilities.

Dr. Mallory addressed the graduates and was well recognized and highly esteemed for her accomplishments in the community. She was honored by community officials for her many years of service at Saints Junior College.

MEDICAL MISSIONARIES OF THE DELTA

Dr. Dorothy Boulding Ferebee was an audacious, bold visionary who sought to "uplift the race" by using volunteer nurse members of Alpha Kappa Alpha (AKAs)—an elite sorority founded at Howard University in 1908. Fighting racism and gender bias Ferebee traveled to Selma, Alabama in 1963 championing voting rights there. She was much like the COGIC educator and activist Arenia Mallory who considered the cause for racial, educational and gender justice a serious matter and who became partners with Ferebee in the Mississippi health care project. Ward (2001:189) points out that the seven-year Mississippi Health Project directed by Dorothy Ferebee would be one of the most "impressive examples of voluntary health work ever conducted by black physicians in the Jim Crow South, [reaching] thousands of black Mississippians at a time when they had virtually no access to professional medical care." Saints Junior College would become part of the history of this traveling medical clinic.

Dorothy Ferebee, fifth from left, appears with team members in Mississippi

A graduate of Tufts Medical School, Ferebee moved to Washington, DC to begin an internship at Freedmen's Hospital—the only hospital that accepted a female doctor in the Jim Crow South. Her family tree included a judge, lawyers, businessmen, and politicians. Poverty that gripped the nation's capital and poor health conditions impacting mothers and their children compelled her to become a part of the solution bringing about change. Ferebee established a settlement house for African American children in 1930 since day care centers were not accessible to African-American mothers due to segregation and racism. Trained as an obstetrician, she was an advocate for reproductive rights and sex education for young girls during a time when such admonitions were dangerous. She treaded on dangerous grounds that could have been very problematic in terms of the legal and justice system of the day.

One of the most compelling stories of her life involved a traveling medical clinic which she led to the Mississippi Delta along with volunteer AKAs. She directed the Mississippi Health Project that brought health care to sharecroppers during the Depression. Beginning in 1930, each summer until the beginning of World War II, volunteer workers traveled thousands of miles on unpaved roads delivering health care to sharecroppers and their families in extreme poverty-stricken areas. Ward (2001:192) reports that Holmes County was selected as the initial beginning of the Mississippi health project because of dire needs of the people living in an impoverished area with limited medical services. Mallory had initially contacted national president of the AKAs Ida Jackson early on, but would later partner with Ferebee in the health care initiative at the Saints School.

Jackson, a native Mississippian, proposed a summer education program in the rural South to upgrade the educational level of the people. Ward (2001:190) reports that upon hearing about the lives of the people and the inspiring "tales about the sharecropping life...from a group of singers from the Saints School in Lexington, Mississippi," Jackson's proposal to send a delegation of volunteers to Mississippi was approved by the AKA convention. Subsequently, the following year six volunteers traveled to Mississippi for 6 weeks to advance the program. The findings from this experience reported by the AKA volunteers were that the health situation of the poor in Mississippi was appalling. Therefore, the situation would necessitate a health care component for the people *before* an educational program could be successful. The following summer, AKAs appropriated $2,500 to advance the health program and nominated Dorothy Boulding Ferebee as the medical director.

Ferebee had gained a reputation for herself in the medical field and was on staff at both Howard and Tufts Medical schools. In 1935, she was approached by her sorority to head the Mississippi Health Project which would begin its "clinical health care experience" in Holmes County. Initially, the project would be stationed at the Saints School. At that time, the School had adequate facilities to accommodate the staff coming from Washington, D.C. However, Ferebee proposed modification to the School in order to expedite services rendered, thus preparing the school to function as the Mississippi Health Projects' Headquarters. Funding provided would bring electricity to the Saints School in order to enlarge the building and screen the front porch.

The project, however, at Saints School was doomed to fail (i.e., movement of the Mississippi Health Project to another county) from the beginning because of several reasons. Racism and discrimination were some of the key factors. Plantation owners refused to allow tenants to leave the grounds to attend the clinic for fear of the nurses being outside agitators. Therefore, the staff of volunteer nurses had to travel *to* plantations in order to administer service. Ward (2001:195-196) reports Ferebee commented that "the entire county [was a] powerful witness of decay and misery…It is little wonder that a people living in this stifling, consuming heat seem lethargic, drugged…the tenants present a pathetic picture as they stare from fields and doorways with expressions at once stupid, vacant, and void of hope…The children, diseased, deformed, aged and wizened all too soon, return no smiles to one's eager gaze… The women were constantly watched by whites while plantation 'riders' with guns in their belts and leather prods in their boot straps…weav[ed] their horses incessantly close to the clinics, straining their ears to hear what the [staffers] were asking of the sharecroppers."

Although the project was considered a success after the first summer, organizers and the AKAs decided to move the

Mississippi Health Project to a less hostile environment. The constant intimidation and racially charged environment added to the discomfort and frustration of workers in addition to the deplorable health conditions in Holmes County. Movement of the project the following year to Bolivar County proved to be less stressful and more progressive in terms of accomplishing the goals set by the project administrator and staff.

HEALTH CARE CENTERS

A significant community-building initiative is named in honor of Dr. Mallory. There are community health centers located in various cities and counties throughout Mississippi, e.g., Canton, Durant, Greenwood, Lexington, and Tchula. .Named the Dr. Arenia C. Mallory Community Health Center(s) (MCHC), the MCHCs were established in 1993 to honor the memory of Dr. Mallory. The mission and vision statements listed at the health care website follow:

The Dr. Arenia C. Mallory Community Health Center, Inc. Board of Directors, Medical Staff, Allied Health Care Professionals, Management Team, and volunteers are committed to the leadership in the delivery of health care services for the residents of Holmes, Carrol counties and surrounding communities. Also included for services is the state of Missouri. Centers provide services such as family planning, pregnancy testing, perinatal care, immunizations, tobacco cessation, counseling, health education and referral services. Services rendered also include medical, dental, pediatric care, OB/GYN, behavior health, and acknowledgement of support from the AstraZeneca HealthCare Foundation in recognition of Dr. Mallory's concern for health care.

The slogan for the center is: "Enter A Patient, Leave A Friend". The slogan reflects the caring which is intrinsic to our mission. Every person who seeks care will be welcomed, comforted, and assisted by our collective talents without regard to financial status. We shall hold in trust the confidential relationship between patient and provider.

We shall work to prevent illnesses, to promote wellness, and to compassionately heal all in our care. We shall be mindful of our responsibility as a community resource and endeavor to enhance the quality of life for every member of our community. The Dr. Arenia C. Mallory Community Health Centers pledge to work with its patients and community as Partners in Excellence to strive to Widening Circles for Health Care Services in Central Mississippi.

Her words resound in one clinic today which is established in Lexington, Mississippi. No doubt Mallory's experiences in building Saints Junior College and her efforts concerning the suffering of children and sharecropping families motivated those who adopted her philosophy to give honor to a woman who had devoted her entire life to benefit others.

PROFESSIONAL MEMBERSHIPS AND HONORS

Dr. Mallory had numerous professional association memberships. There is an enormous list of activities and events covering her entire life. Some of her noted accomplishments and honors listed in a Congressional Record in Mississippi follow:

HONORING THE CITY OF LEXINGTON, MISSISSIPPI

HON. BENNIE G. THOMPSON
Of Mississippi in the House of Representatives

Thursday, June 19, 2014

Mr. THOMPSON of Mississippi. Mr. Speaker, I rise today to acknowledge the historically rich city of Lexington, Mississippi.

Lexington is a city in Holmes County, Mississippi. The population was 2,025 as of the 2000 census. It was named in honor of Lexington, Massachusetts. Like much of the state, Holmes County suffered during and after the Civil War. The City of Lexington is served by the Holmes County School District. It is also served by a private school called Central Holmes Christian School (formerly Central Holmes Academy).

The City of Lexington also has some rich African-American History. It is the root for the Church of God in Christ (COGIC) (formerly called the Church of God when it got its Lexington beginning) by founder Bishop Charles Harrison Mason.

The City of Lexington can also boast as having the first black-elected school superintendent in the State of Mississippi--Elder William Dean, who is now pastor of the St. Paul Church of God in Christ here in Lexington. The church is situated next to the beautiful campus of Saints College (now closed to students) but is used for multiple purposes, especially its church-like edifice commonly known as ``Holy Hill.''

Saints College was founded by an African-American, Dr. Arenia Mallory as Saints Industrial and Literary School. The historically black school was renamed and is currently called Saints Academy. Dr. Mallory served as president of the school from 1926 until her death in 1983. It is run under the Church of God in Christ. Dr. Mallory was an active member of the COGIC church and participated in the Women's Department and was the leader in the national church. She also served as the Vice President of the National Council of Negro Women from 1953-1957.

Lexington is also the home of the Dr. Arenia C. Mallory Community Health Center, Inc. (Mallory CHC) founded by Dr. Martha Davis (now deceased). Its mission is to provide high quality, customer oriented and cost effective healthcare services in a safe and accessible environment to all persons of Holmes, Carroll, Madison, Leflore counties and surrounding communities. Its motto is ``Enter a Patient, Leave a Friend.'' (See more about the clinic at **http://www.mallorychc.org/**)

The City of Lexington is also the home of the Community Students Learning Center (CSLC) founded by longtime African-American natives Leslie and Beulah Greer: ``Our Mission for the Community Students Learning Center is to promote community and educational change, by providing state-of-the-art leadership development and personal improvement opportunities for youth, adults, and seniors.'' Its motto is

"In Relentless Pursuit of Education and Knowledge. (See more about CSLC at: http://www.communitystudentlearning.org/)

The City of Lexington was at the heart of the Civil Rights Movement in Holmes County, Mississippi. Brave men and women, black and white, protested, challenged and worked hard to bring about racial harmony.

While some success in that regard was made, the city and County both still could currently use more racial reconciliation, according to some of the residents.

In addition to numerous historical firsts, today, the City of Lexington also boasts first ever Black Mayor of Lexington, Mississippi--the Honorable Mayor Clint Cobbins, who is currently leading his community toward progress.

Mr. Speaker, I ask my colleagues to join me in recognizing the City of Lexington as a resilient, historically rich rural town that has maintained its community ties inside and outside its city limits by staying true to its roots in agriculture and local owned businesses.

Goodson (2016) also cites honors and awards Dr. Mallory received during her lifetime:

- Selected by the National Council of Negro Women as one of the 9 "Outstanding Women in America" in 1940 and 1956, citing her contribution as an "Educator and Leader of Women"
- Appointed by the Department of Labor to serve as Manpower Specialist and Consultant for the Labor Department, Washington, DC
- Received Merit Award for contribution in education
- Cited by the International Church Of God In Christ, November, 1969
- The first person of color and first woman to be elected to the Holmes County Board of Education in Mississippi
- Appears in Who's Who of American Women's Biographical

Dictionary of Notable Living American Women
- Charter/Life member of Nat'l Council of Negro Women
- Traveled throughout the world with her election in 1952 as the only female delegate of the Church Of God In Christ to the Pentecostal Convention in London, England
- Delegate to the Tenth celebration of the United Nations in San Francisco in 1956. This occasion was marked by the presence of many foreign delegates
- Received the Governor's Outstanding Mississippi Award from Governor Waller who proclaimed April 19, as Arenia C. Mallory day in the entire State of Mississippi
- Awarded the Degree of Doctor of Humanities by South Eastern University in Greenville, South Carolina
- Cited by the Church Civic League of Cleveland, Ohio in 1968 as being among Women of Achievement at the Manager Hotel
- Cited by the National Association for the Advancement of Colored People
- Honored among the top twelve women in government by Delta Sigma Theta sorority in 1966
- Associated with various professional and civic organizations such as the Administration of Rural Education; Southern Conference on Human Relations; The Women's Organization of Higher Education; National Society for the Prevention of Juvenile Delinquency which she served as president

SUMMARY AND CONCLUSIONS

It was the wisdom of God, imbued in her spirit, that called forth norms and values of Black culture while guiding Mallory's life that predestined her to freedom fight, advocate, uplift, witness, testify, and become the driving for of a school in Lexington, Mississippi for 50 years! Her beliefs were grounded in an unmovable faith in God and an assurance that she would be an overcomer in spite of all the difficulties and odds.

Dr. Mallory was surrounded by a brutal and violent history of events tainting the literary accounts of the era. Such tragedies perhaps may have left some individuals unforgiving especially when questions remained unanswered where justice did not prevail. Grim remembrances mark events such as the murder of Emmett Till in Money, Mississippi in 1955; the murder of Medgar Evers in Jackson, Mississippi in 1963; and the murder in Neshoba County, Mississippi in 1964, of three civil rights individuals—Andrew Goodman, James Chaney, and Michael Schwerner who were working on the "Freedom Summer" campaign attempting to register voters. Mississippi was the focus of civil rights activism for Freedom Summer. In view of the fact there was an ongoing effort by activists engaged in improving race relations and helping to bring about social change in Mississippi communities, progress was very slow.

In addition to Mississippi's dark history, other aspects of various Delta counties suffered under the grip of racism and segregation. Wynveen (2009:213) reports that "Mississippi has a long-standing [history] as one of the least healthy states in the country." High rates of poverty, poor medical health facilities, lack of health care providers, (particularly in rural areas), low levels of education, and health related illness such as cardiovascular disease have continued to exist in counties included in the Mississippi Delta. Chronic illnesses have also plagued this area due to the lack of adequate health care facilities and protocols.

Wynveen (2009:216) points out that according to the U.S. census in 2000, several of the Mississippi Delta counties in her study reveal a high minority presence and low household incomes. For example, Holmes County is reported as having a population of about 21,500, a median household income of about $17,200, and 78.7% African-American. The data give a clear picture of disadvantage in Holmes County alone and evidence to support the cruel reality that Dr. Mallory must have encountered in attempting to change the educational and economic situation for rural sharecroppers and their families. Yet she was able to rise above the difficulties she faced during that time. Perhaps she gained strength from the scripture, noted by Simmons & Martin (1983:41): "Lo, I am with you always."

This writer visited the campus of Saints Junior College and beheld its splendor and beauty. At the time of the visit, however, buildings were empty and the Deborah Mason Patterson/Arenia C. Mallory Multi-Purpose Building sat alone on Holy Hill—as it was named. Inside contained some artifacts and pictures on the wall of saints who had been laid to rest. It seemed strange that there was no life on the campus. So many young people had once walked on these grounds and now there were only buildings in memory of the president who had given her life for this school.

It is no wonder that when Bishop L.H. Ford served as the Presiding Bishop of the Churches Of God In Christ that he called for immediate re-opening of the school which had closed in 1983 and remains closed as of this writing.

One final mention in this essay concerning Dr. Mallory's involvement is noted in support of her multi-faceted vision for educational development. Educational programs were sponsored by Saints Junior College focusing on an environmental education series on early childhood education, race and cultural education, health education and religious education. The National Endowment for the Humanities was the sponsoring grantee to Saints Junior College which presented these series via WXTN. The August 1973 *Holmes County Herald* reports that the title of this program was "Environmental Education in Mississippi as a State and Holmes County." One of the instructors for the program was from Saints Junior College. This was one of the many efforts that Mallory was involved in developing and influencing the culture in Holmes County and the state of Mississippi.

The life of Dr. Mallory and the impact she made on the society and culture is replete with unheard testimonials. One can imagine the magnitude of her accomplishments. The breadth and depth of her service is beyond measure. Truly she was an ambassador for justice; an advocate for educational advancement; a champion for the cause of civil rights; an activist in government service; a supporter of health care providers for all in need; and a spokesperson for economic empowerment for all people, particularly African-Americans. Let us not end her life story in the words of a letter written to Harriet Tubman from Frederick Douglass in 1868:

I have had the applause of the crowd and the satisfaction that comes of being approved by the multitude, while the most that you have done has been witnessed by...scarred,...bondmen and women, whom you have led out of the house of bondage, and whose heartfelt "God bless you" has been your only reward. The midnight sky and the silent stars have been the witness of your devotion to freedom and of your heroism.....

It is only until we are able to uncover the untold stories and added accounts of Dr. Mallory's life, that we can have a more substantive and complete record of her various contributions to church and society, her impact on culture and the "Grand Old Church Of God In Christ!"

Except from Glimpses

Some Organizations and Honors Dr. Mallory Received Honor and Held Membership

Projecting her career from the Mississippi Delta to the National and International scene, Dr. Mallory has become affiliated with many professional, religious, and civic organizations. These include the Academy of Political Science; American Teacher's Association, National Education Association; Administration of Rural Education; Southern Conference on Human Relations; The Women's Organization of Higher Education; and the National Society for the Prevention of Juvenile Delinquency in which she served as Vice President.

Dr. Mallory was selected by the National Council of Negro Women as one of the nine "Outstanding Women of America" in 1940 and in 1956, citing her contribution as an "Educator and leader of Women." The Utility Club of New York City design[at]ed her as "Woman of the Year." Sharing honors with Congressman Adam Clayton Powell, Jr. – the Utility Club's "Man of the Year." Dr. Mallory received her award in the presence of 1500 guests assembled at ceremonies in New York's Waldorf Astoria Hotel.

National Council of Negro Women

A charter and life member of the National Council of Negro Women, Dr. Malory was a regional Director for eight years, during which period she organized the Southern Regional meetings for the States of Alabama, Arkansas, Florida, Louisiana, Mississippi, Oklahoma and Texas. She was first Vice President of National Council of Negro Women for four years; in 1954, she was the delegate of the Council at the Convention of Women in Helsinki, Finland and immediately following this occasion, she was guest of the Swedish Council of Women.

National Council of Women of the United States

During many years of service to the National Council of Women of the United States which the National Council of Negro Women is affiliated and which, in turn, is affiliated with the International Council of Women, Dr. Mallory has on several occasions represented this organization at the International level. In 1956, she was a delegate to the Tenth celebration of the United Nations in San Francisco, where she spoke on the program of the Merchandise Mart, an occasion significantly marked by the presence of many Foreign delegates.

She became Vice President of the National Council of Women of the United States in 1956; as its delegate and member of its Educational Commission of the International Council of Women in Montreal, Canada in 1956.

Honored in April, 1968, by the Chicago Alumni of Saints Junior College at the Dunbar High School Auditorium.

In October, 1973, Dr. Mallory was awarded the Degree of Doctor of Humanities by South Eastern University, Greenville, SC.

In November, 1973, Dr. Mallory was cited by the Church of God in Christ, International, during the Convocation.

On April 19, 1974, The Board of Supervisors of Holmes County named Castalian Road "Arenia C. Mallory Road."

In November, 1974, Dr. Mallory was re-selected to the Holmes County Board of Education for another six-year term.

White House Participation

Dr. Mallory's participated in many state, national, and International conferences including the White House Conference on Children and Youth, and the White House Conference on the Aging.

Teacher housing, 1963 Eagles, Staff Members, Celebrating 41 years of Service, Saints Band Members 1974, Leaving Chapel

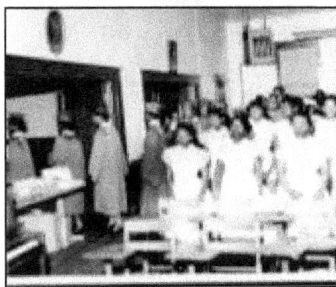

Bookstore, With Mary McCloud Bethune and National Council of Negro Women Washington, D.C., 1967 Choir, Track and Field, Graduation, Social gathering

Chapter 5

Dr. Mallory on Overseas Tour

Dr. Mallory as a 20th Century Model: THE SERVICE AND SACRIFICE OF WOMEN GOING INTO THE EVERYWHERE

June Rivers

Only those who can see the invisible can do the impossible. Albert Einstein

The recurring theme in the Gospels is that of service and sacrifice. In Mark 10:45, Christ says, "For even the Son of Man did not come to be served, but to serve, and to give His life as a ransom for many (NKJV)." Dr. Mallory exemplified the life of Christ through her life of service and sacrifice, even suffering persecution. Dr. Mallory was not a second, third, or fourth generation COGIC member as some of us profess in a prideful manner. However, when 17 year old Arenia Mallory rolled in the sawdust in her beautiful ruffled dress at a tent revival and received the Baptism of the Holy Spirit, she embraced the tenets of the COGIC, and committed her life to service and sacrifice for over 50 years. She disobeyed her mother and returned to the COGIC revival, rejecting her mother's dream for her to become a concert pianist and joined the "crazy sanctified folks."

At age 21 'Dad' Mason recruited her to teach music at Saints Industrial in Lexington, Mississippi rather than pursuing her dream of going to Africa. At this young age, Arenia wanted to serve and already she had experienced sacrifices. Sometime after her arrival Mr. Courts, the school administrator, died and Mallory was appointed principal by 'Dad' Mason. She encountered persecution and racism from the town's citizens, both Black and White, and the men of the church because she was a northerner and a woman, who was light skinned. Despite challenges and obstacles, she developed Saints from a school in deplorable condition into an educational institution that could compete with any Historically Black College of that era. Dr. Mallory channeled her God given talents and skills cultivated in her middle class upbringing to improving the quality of life and education at Saints. Such an accomplishment catapulted COGIC from a 'church sect' to a religion.

Ms. Mallory was a phenomenal and extraordinary woman willing to make sacrifices in her personal life in order to achieve the vision that God had given her. "This independent, missions-minded streak in Mallory would be both a blessing and

Saints Student Annie C. Wah of Liberia

a curse later in her personal life and future dealings with COGIC leadership." (Butler 2007:101) She established a legacy for us to emulate. Her dedication to providing quality education for youth, her concern for the issues of the world, and her partnerships with individuals, organizations, and governments, who assisted her in achieving her goals, left a road map for us to follow. One need only interview former students at Saints Industrial Junior College to measure her success in educating thousands. There are men and women who have accomplished great feats not only in COGIC but in the secular world as well. In addition to Saints rigorous curriculum for a number of years, numerous extra curricula activities were available. A life of sanctification was the foundation of the school. Students learned to fast, pray, and operate in the gifts of the Spirit. They learned in their youth about faith in God and the many aspects of ministry. Ms. Mallory's life of service yielded much fruit along with the many painful sacrifices that she suffered.

She was a visionary whose commitment to service resulted in her forming numerous partnerships to solve issues of women and education at home and abroad. Mother Lizzie Robinson did not approve of joining organizations and participating in politics, believing that we were to be in the world but not of the world. However, Ms. Mallory was not deterred by such disapproval. She travelled abroad nationally and internationally as a member in various women's organizations, as a conference representative, and in the interest of missions. In some of the organizations which sought to bring solutions to the issues of Black women as well as all women on an international scale, she held key leadership roles. Ms. Mallory was a charter member of the National Council of Negro Women (NCNW) founded by Mary McLeod Bethune. Ms. Mallory and Ms. Bethune became personal friends because of their missionary spirit and life of holiness. Both wanted to go to Africa but Ms. Bethune was not allowed to go because she was Black. Also, they shared a common desire to provide quality education for poor Blacks.

Dr. Mallory's concern for quality education extended even to the continent of Africa. After her return from Liberia, West Africa, she formed an organization to raise funds to bring students from the interior of their country to the United States for more advanced educational opportunities. Some of these students went on to provide great service both to the Church Of God In Christ and also to their country. One such student, Bishop Amos Nyema, at this writing is the current prelate of the Liberian Jurisdiction. The late Bishop Abraham Brown was the prelate of the Côte d'Ivoire (Ivory Coast) Jurisdiction. Prior to becoming a Bishop, Abraham Brown and his wife Jesse maintained the school and church property at the Monolu Station in the interior of Liberia that was established by Missionary Elizabeth White, the first COGIC missionary to Africa in 1929. Missionary Francina Wiggins continued the work that Mother White started. God orders our steps so that we can fulfill His divine plan.

While I do not consider myself to be as distinguished as Dr.

Mallory in ultimate service and sacrifice, I was an educator for 35 years and I have served as Coordinator and then Director of Youth On A Mission (YOAM) since 1989 leading teams of youth and adults to an international country every summer in July. My involvement in missions comes from the legacy of my maternal grandmother, Alberta Vinson Green and my father, Havious Vinson Green. This God ordained work in missions was confirmed in the prophetic reasons of my mother who identified why I should consider Charles (Chuck) Rivers as a husband. At the time, I only thought of Chuck as a friend who impressed me because as an African American male, he knew so much about other cultures and related so well to the international students at the university we attended. Together, we spearheaded several university wide activities to celebrate Black History month with the involvement of international students, especially from the continent of Africa. I did not know that God had planned for my husband and me to take teams around the world for the Church Of God In Christ. I rejected Chuck for his religious background and his unique personality. However, God did not reject him and had selected him to carry out the work of missions with his wife. I chose to heed my mother's prophesy even though my sisters and I did not consider my mother as a woman with a prophetic gift. God is so awesome in that He has a plan for us if we are willing to say yes, send me. God orders our steps so that we can fulfill His divine plan.

My grandmother became an active missions' supporter in the thirties. After hearing the testimonies of the missionaries, Alberta Vinson Green secured clothing from Hudson's Department Store (now Macy's) and books from a suburban Detroit School District which were sent in trunks to Haiti and Liberia. To pay the shipping costs, my grandmother's sons sold her homemade pies for ten cents. My grandmother was a member of the stewardess board and a State Counselor of Volunteer Missions for Michigan during the administration of Mother Lillian Brooks Coffey, who was the International Supervisor of the Women's Department for the Church Of God In Christ and the President of the Women's International Convention.

The Home and Foreign Missions work was established by our first International Supervisor Lizzie Robinson. The Home and Foreign mission worked in three phases: 1) the directors of missions were women who carried on the mission work in the state through organized Home and Foreign mission bands; 2) the stewardess board were women who worked exclusively to package clothing, foodstuffs for foreign fields and to distribute to institutions at home, tracts, Bibles, candy, fruit, and other items; 3) the counselors of volunteer missions were women who carried full-time mission programs through interested volunteers." Women's International Convention Souvenir Journal and Program, May 7-12, 1957). My grandmother had nine children and minimum income but she served and sacrificed despite her poverty as did many of the COGIC women during this time. God ordered her steps so that she could fulfill His divine plan through her.

Mother Coffey expanded the legacy of missions work established Mother Robinson. In 1951, Mother Coffey, with the approval of Bishop Mason, initiated the Women's Convention to financially support missions and the missionaries abroad. The 1957 Women's Convention Souvenir Journal displays a picture of Mother Coffey and other women disembarking a train in San Diego for the 1956 Women's Convention. My grandmother, who was an ardent supporter of Mother Coffey and the missions work, is shown in this picture. Mother Coffey purchased a luxurious home at 154 Arden Park in Detroit, Michigan as a place where missionaries could go and rest. Mother Green was actively involved in raising funds to purchase the Lillian Brooks Coffey Rest Home. (Mother Coffey also had several such houses in other cities.)

My father Elder Havious Green, an educator, talked about a colleague who traveled to Ghana to work as a teacher. These conversations sparked my interest in traveling abroad. When I became an adult, my father began a lifetime of traveling internationally to Haiti, Democratic Republic of Congo, and other countries, sometimes traveling with Mother Mary Beth and the late Elder Charles Kennedy, who served as missionaries in Liberia. He later traveled with Youth On A Mission. Elder Green gave hundreds of thousands of dollars to various missions' projects such as building schools, churches, clinics, and orphanages around the world. He paid for the building of houses for indigenous pastors and bishops and paid the salaries of teachers in various countries. God ordered Pastor Green's steps so that he could fulfill His divine plan.

Church of God in Christ leaders have traveled the globe since the organization's earliest days. Dr. Mallory attended the Pentecostal World Conference in London, England in 1952 as a member of the Church Of God In Christ delegation. Little is written about Bishop Charles Harrison Mason's international travels, however, he spoke at this conference while thousands of Caucasians stood in rapt attention. Then Bishop Mason journeyed on to Israel, where in 2015 a group of Christian Ethiopian Jewish churches joined COGIC.

The work of my grandmother and my father stirred my desire

to travel for the church. In 1982, my husband and I attended the Pentecostal World Conference in Nairobi, Kenya. It had been my dream for years to go to this conference when it was on the continent of Africa. The Lord worked a miracle! A two week teacher strike delayed the start of school in the month of September which allowed me, an assistant principal, time off to attend. We met Bishop Carlis L. Moody, who was president of the Missions Department, and the host of the COGIC group traveling to Kenya. This experience was our inauguration into the world of missions. I went to Liberia as a member of YOAM in 1984 and in 1989 Bishop Moody appointed me as YOAM Coordinator. Each summer we take groups of youth and adults for two weeks to a country where there are Churches Of God In Christ. The team engages in five ministries: construction, evangelism, hospitality, medical, and Vacation Bible School. In 1990, my husband, our daughter, who was eleven months old, and I took a YOAM team to Brazil. God orders our steps so that we can fulfill His divine plan.

The Church Of God In Christ is presently in over 80 countries around the world, many of which are under developed. Some of our churches are in the villages where children have to walk miles to get to the nearest government school. In some countries, children are snatched by the witch doctor or taken for ransom. In other countries, men believe that having sex with a virgin will protect them from AIDS, therefore it is not safe for girls to walk a long distance to school. Dr. Mallory was concerned about the quality of education in the interior of Liberia in 1960 and fifty-six years later there is not a high school in the interior. The Honorable Alexander Gbayee, Consul General of Liberia, a member of COGIC who was brought to the U.S. by Missionary Martha Barber, has established the Liberian Hope Foundation to raise funds for building a Vocational and College Preparatory High School for Tugbaken in the southeast region of Maryland County. There are both church and government primary schools in the interior. The Church Of God In Christ was established in Liberia circa 1929. What a travesty, eighty-seven years later, the children in the interior of Liberia do not have the opportunity of secondary education in 2016. God orders our steps so that we can fulfill His divine plan.

In my secular profession, I was an educator in such capacities as teacher, reading specialist, a school administrator, and a central office administrator over the K-12 Literacy Department for a large urban district. The opportunities and experiences that I had as an educator were awesome. In 1996, I was a Milken Family Foundation National Educator Award Recipient and received a gift of $25,000. I used the funds to finance the building of a church in Guyana, South America and to purchase a sign for the front of the school where I was principal. God blessed me to be recognized by the secular community for my service and sacrificial life to education. Due to my years of experience as an educator and from my Child Evangelism Fellowship Training, the YOAM team and I have worked each year to improve the quality of our Vacation Bible School program. We use five colors along with corresponding Scriptures to teach the plan of salvation so that anyone can understand it in spite of any language barrier. The YOAM team and my family have taken the gospel of Jesus Christ to thousands of children and youth in many countries. God orders our steps so that we can fulfill His divine plan.

In our travels abroad, especially to the villages, we envisioned the need for five pillars to strengthen the infrastructure of these communities. The five pillars are churches, schools and dormitories (orphanages), clinics, water wells, and sustainable community development. In 2004, YOAM partnered with Habitat for Humanity (HFH) to build houses in the Philippines' interior. The HFH staff were shocked that we could clear the land of trees and foliage, make bricks, dig four foundations, and build a house in one week. We accomplished more than any group that HFH had in the past.

In 2006, YOAM worked to complete the building of several churches in Malawi. In one village, the team slept on dirt floors for two nights in homes that did not have any plumbing for toilets or electricity for lights. At one church location, we built the tresses for the roof and then the taller team members hoisted them up one at a time to the Malawians to secure them in place. We were informed that before the church would be completed the membership would outgrow the building. The headquarters church had started a school in its facility without educational materials and supplies, or adequately trained teachers. The educators on the team and I met with the pastor and his staff about how to best train the teachers.

In 2012, the YOAM medical team trained the staff at a Ugandan village clinic and left materials and medical supplies.

In 2014, the YOAM team travelled across two rivers, one rapidly moving, in a canoe, up the side of the mountain into a rain forest to visit the BriBri Indian tribe who had recently become Christians. We took pipes so that water could flow from the mountain into the village. The pillar that needs development is to train villagers in skills that will help them build sustainable economies. God faithfully orders our steps so that we can fulfill His divine plan.

There are women in the Church Of God In Christ today whose life of service and sacrifice parallel that of Dr. Mallory's. This essay includes four who answered the call to serve around the world and, like Mallory, have formed partnerships to achieve their God directed goals. Contemporary international supervisors, they have done great exploits at home and in the countries where they serve: Supervisors Maddaline Norfleet, Herldleen Russell, Emma Rose Sanders, and Lee Etta Van Zandt. These women were not supervisors when they began their journey but became supervisors as a result of their work. Not only are they international supervisors but three of them serve or have served as supervisors of jurisdictions. I met these distinguished women in my work with the Department of World Missions. I have had the honor of travelling internationally with three of the four women so I have personally observed their commitment and sacrifices.

There is a documentary entitled, *Iron Ladies of Liberia*, which chronicles the first year Ellen Johnson-Sirleaf served as the president of Liberia, West Africa and the first elected female president in Africa. These women that I interviewed for this chapter are "Iron Ladies" as well. They have encountered numerous challenges and have overcome immeasurable odds to accomplish the work of the Lord. I would also compare them to Harriet Tubman who endangered her life to bring enslaved people from the grips of slavery in the South to a life of freedom in the North. Ms. Tubman feared no one. Often, I have been asked if I am ever afraid in my international travels for COGIC. I have experienced the faithfulness of God and so I am cautious but never afraid. Tongue in cheek, I remind people that I live in an urban city, Detroit, that at one time was the murder capital of America. However, God created me to be a risk taker and so I am exhilarated by the adventure of travel. God has been faithful in all of our travels working out all situations that we encounter. We travelled to Liberia in 2000 and there were still rival military groups in the interior opposing the presidency of President Charles Taylor. Soldiers detained us for hours at the border between the Ivory Coast and Liberia. The list goes on of all the dangers that we have encountered but God has protected us. God orders our steps so that we will fulfill His divine plan which requires sacrifice.

There were three questions or statements that I posed to these "Iron Ladies" of God. These women were to

- *describe childhood experiences that propelled them into a life of service;*
- *discuss in detail their mission work giving dates for key events;*
- *discuss partnerships that they formed in order to achieve the goals and objectives of their work.*

IRON LADIES OF THE CHURCH OF GOD IN CHRIST

Maddaline Ann Jenkins Norfleet

Maddaline Norfleet is a third generation COGIC woman. Her grandparents, Deacon Alexander and Minnie Lewis received salvation in the Church Of God In Christ in the year 1919. Her mother and father separated when she was two years old leaving her mom with three small children to raise alone. Her father actually told her mother, *"I never wanted children"* and one day he left. Being the only girl, her mother kept her close by her side. She didn't go to dances, proms or sleepovers. Church was their lives and everything they did somehow evolved around the church.

Maddaline received the Baptism of the Holy Ghost two months after her 10th birthday at her home church, Richardson

Memorial COGIC in Waterbury, Connecticut in a New Year's revival conducted by the State Supervisor, Mother Rebekah E. Gorham. As a young girl, Maddaline's mother would keep her home from school to serve with the state hospitality hostesses on Women's Day of the Holy Convocations and Spring Conferences. It was during that time that her love for serving people was birthed and cultivated. She loved everything that had to do with hospitality and serving people. Her mother would say to her, *"Maddaline, the Lord put a servant's heart in you for a reason"* and add, *"I may never go anywhere, but God is gonna use you and send you all over the world to help people."* At the time Maddaline couldn't imagine what God was speaking into her mother's spirit about her little girl. At bedtime her mother would kneel down bedside her bedside and teach Maddaline how to pray. She would say, *"Maddaline, when you pray the Lord is gonna show you things and I don't want you to be afraid to do what he tells you. He's gonna let you see faces of people you don't know and hear voices of people you can't understand because he wants you to go and help them".* She'd say, *"I want you to see your prayers going over the ocean and into countries where they don't know God and pray for them to get saved."* At the time Maddaline had no idea that the Lord was using her Mom, an uneducated, single parent to steer her into a life of mission work.

Later, being married with children of her own, Maddaline settled into what seemed to be a really nice life for herself. She had a beautiful home, a saved successful husband who loved her, and a great job working for a Fortune 500 Pharmaceutical Company. What more could she ask for? It was around that time that she and her husband began attending the Azusa Conferences in Tulsa, Oklahoma. Each year she was drawn to the missions' classes taught by a diminutive Caucasian woman named Pastor Sharon. Maddaline was captivated by her fascinating missions' stories of helping people around the world. For three or four years she approached Pastor Sharon after class and say, *"I would like to go on a mission trip with you"*, Pastor Sharon responded with a smile and say, *"Oh, I don't know if you'd like it very much, maybe you should give a donation instead."* She said that because Maddaline was always dressed up with big shinny hats and rings on every other finger. She thought Maddaline was too delicate and girly for the *Real Mission Field*. One day, out of the blue, Maddaline received a letter from Pastor Sharon inviting her to accompany her on a missions' trip to India. It was on that trip that Pastor Sharon shared how God showed her that she would be a devoted missionary for him and that she had misjudged her.

After that trip, Pastor Sharon took her along on many missions' trips around the world. Whenever they went to a new country to minister the gospel she would introduce Maddaline by saying, *"This is Missionary Maddaline Norfleet and she's going to do what I've been doing for the past 40 years, RECEIVE HER!"* After she said that she would sit down, fold her arms across her chest and watch Maddaline.

Pastor Sharon would often tell her that she was a _book of matches_ for Christ but Maddaline would be a _blowtorch for him_, burning a path through the nations that leads straight to Jesus Christ. According to Maddaline, Pastor Sharon "poured over 40 years of experience into me." They went to places that heard about Christ and places that had not. They organized medical mission clinics with indigenous doctors and nurses as well as those from the USA along with volunteers. Some of the places where they lodged were simply awful but it was the only place available for them to stay. The Lord gave Maddaline an incredible grace to deal with bugs, animals, obnoxious odors, little or no running water and all of the things that would send the average Pentecostal church girl running back to the U.S., never to return. But, the more she saw the more she wanted to see. The more challenging the trip the deeper the passion for missions grew inside of her. Many of her friends were perplexed as to why she would choose to leave the niceties of home, church and country to subject herself to the discomforts of the mission's field. All she could say was, *"God called me to it."*

In 2004, by the leading of the Lord and a great deal of encouragement from her husband, Pastor Joseph Norfleet, she established *"Grace Like Rain World Missions,"* a subsidiary of her local church, Faith Center in Meriden, CT. G.L.R.W.M. was birthed out of the many needs she saw as she traveled on the missions' field over the years. Missionary Maddaline had read about the bold accomplishments of Dr. Arenia Conelia Mallory who never looked at a need and saw the restrictions but looked at a need and envisioned the possibilities. As a result, by the grace of God and help from anywhere God would allow, she has been able to accomplish the following:

In 2005, the Lady Maddaline's Children Home (L.M.C.H.) was founded by she and her husband in Guntur, India in response to the December 2004 South East Asian Tsunami. There are presently over 80 children living at L.M.C.H. ranging from the ages of 4 to 17. The home has two houses adjacent to each other, one for girls and one for boys, four paid staff and several volunteers. With support from COGIC World Missions, the India 4th Jurisdiction and several other nondenominational ministries, all the needs of the children are met including school tuition, medical needs, and daily necessities.

In 2008, the Grace Like Rain New Hope Training Center for

the Blind was founded. Missionary Maddaline met a young man in Kampala, Uganda who brought her to his mother who was blind from birth. This woman lived 1½ hours from Kampala in a small house left to her by her deceased husband. She had taken in five totally blind girls, ages 18 to 25 from a nearby village. The woman taught them how to hand weave colored straw into baskets, floor mats, tabletops and other household items. After witnessing the work the woman was doing all alone, Maddaline was in tears. She didn't know how she was going to do it, but she knew that God was leading her to help this woman start a training center for the blind. Soon thereafter, the GLR New Living Hope Training Center for the Blind was established, with Missionary Maddaline as the overseer.

Undergirded by her local church and other monthly contributors, they were able to purchase materials and equipment for the school, as well as house, clothe and feed the student trainees. Each blind student in the program is there for approximately two years and upon completion of the training, they are able to join the workforce making and selling their crafts at the public market. In 2015, the school found favor with a wealthy Ugandan woman who donated much of the funds needed to build a brand new facility. In March of 2016 Maddaline traveled to Uganda to dedicate the new school. At the present time, the new facility houses fifteen students and six staff.

In 2011 the Grace Tailoring and Training Institute was established in India by Femina Bezwada and Missionary Maddaline. It is a training program developed to help extremely impoverished and abused women who work in the fields for little more than one dollar per day. The women had no skills or education so they were limited to working in the fields making barely enough to feed themselves or their children. One day, Missionary Maddaline sat at Femina's kitchen table in India and dreamed aloud of a program that could stop the cycle of poverty and establish these women in business for themselves. They hired a professional seamstress to teach the women how to sew on foot-powered sewing machines. Now, 35 to 50 women are taken from the fields every 6 months and taught tailoring, design skills and techniques. The women that do well in the program are rewarded with a sewing machine to either work in an existing tailoring shop or start their own business. Many of the graduates from the program come back to the school to help teach new trainees. To date eleven classes have graduated and many, many sewing machines are given away. The funds to purchase the sewing machines, supplies and to pay for teaching staff comes from people all over the USA who hear about the program and *sow into the lives of those who sew*. In 2016, Mother Vanessa Macklin, wife of our Second Assistant Presiding Bishop J.W. Macklin and the women of their local church gave the project the largest contribution ever received of 36 brand new foot-powered sewing machines.

In 2011, the Little Angels Primary School was established. The school starts at the nursery school level and goes through the 3rd grade. The children are taught in the English language and their native language of Telugu. This school is comprised of children from the Hindu, Muslim and Christian communities.

The examination scores of the children attending the school are so high that the parents of non-Christian families have no problem paying a small tuition for their child to attend. The school incorporates strong Christian values and teachings through songs, stories and Bible Scriptures into the curriculum. As a result, the children go home from school and teach their parents about Christ. It is a "*Win, Win*" situation. The rest of the funding for the school comes from charitable donations from the Indian community and USA contributors.

In 2013, the Grace Like Rain Mar Atin School in Oyam, Northern Uganda was established. The school is comprised of students at the Pre-K level through 6th grade. While ministering at a church in one of the large cities in Uganda, a female associate minister told Missionary Maddaline of the plight of her native village. Due to Warlords who had settled in the area, the people of Oyam District were afraid to send their children to school. As a result, the schools shut down and the children no longer received an education. After a ten year occupation, the Ugandan government was successful at ridding the area of the Warlords but still there were no schools. This minister had 30 acres of land given to her by her family and felt a burden to build a school on it. She came to Maddaline and asked if she would prayerfully consider partnering with her to find teachers, the funding to build, and support the school. By the grace of God, Maddaline found the funds and began to build one classroom at a time. Now the school provides education to over 400 children with licensed teachers and a government-approved curriculum. The children are very happy to be in school and are passing their grades with flying colors.

In 2014, Missionary Maddaline was elevated to Supervisor of the Ethiopia Church of God In Christ Jurisdiction to serve with Bishop Corby Bush. Since that time she has been very instrumental in working with the pastors of the jurisdiction and seeking out funds to complete a 1500 seat temple being built in the Jeldu area of Ethiopia, as well as, organizing the women of the Jurisdiction. The new edifice is now complete and it was her joy to travel to Ethiopia in March of 2016 to participate in the dedication festivities and services.

Other areas of missions include <u>Women's Conferences</u>, <u>Discipleship Training</u> and <u>Leadership Conferences</u> that are held every year in various countries. These conferences and training events are held in the Ethiopia, Philippine Islands, India, Thailand, Vietnam, Cambodia, Myanmar, China, Japan, Uganda, Ghana, and Barbados.

Since 2008, she has organized and conducted numerous medical clinics offering services in pediatrics, geriatrics, dental, optical, and general first aid in several countries.

Dr. Herdleen Russell

Dr. Herldleen Russell, the Supervisor of Uganda, East Africa for thirteen years, has had an incredible journey similar to Supervisor Norfleet. Both women were strongly influenced by their mothers, formed partnerships outside of COGIC, and went wherever God called. Herldleen's foundation for service and sacrifice came from the example of her mother, Bessie Lott. Her mother was widowed when Herldleen was 3 years old. Mrs. Lott was left with six children, four under ten years of age, and Herldleen was the youngest. It was 1947 and segregation was firmly entrenched even in Chicago, Illinois where the Lott family lived. Mrs. Lott's desire to purchase a home for her children, took her to bank after bank for a mortgage and she was repeatedly turned down. Her tenacity, fortitude, and trust in her God, motivated her to continue despite the numerous rejections. Finally, one banker said to her, "Mrs. Lott I need to advise you on the uselessness of your endeavors: 1) You are a woman; 2) You do not have a husband to undergird you so if you fail in this attempt you will have nothing to fall back on; and 3)…(unspoken), you are black." Her mother's response was, "I am not here for charity and I'm not alone. All I'm asking you to do is to give 'my God' and me a chance." He quickly turned the papers around and said, "Sign here." This story and her mother's example throughout Herldleen's life instilled in her that *"I can do all things through Christ who strengthens me,"* Philippians 4:13. She never felt alone. With God, no matter how great the opposition, she and God were in the majority. There was no task too great that her God and she could not achieve. She had learned to trust Him and step out in faith and watch Him work miracles. Herldleen's mother was her example of a visionary who accomplished more impossible things with her God than Herldleen had seen in families with both parents. Mrs. Lott was a world traveler and introduced Herldleen to a world that was greater than her neighborhood or any vacation spot. Herldleen never saw her mother fear anyone or any situation.

Herldleen Lott met her husband Elder Herbert J. Russell at Moody Bible Institute, a school which emphasized Missions. She graduated from this school in 1978. Third generation COGIC, her husband brought Herldleen into this church where sanctification and the power of the Holy Ghost was introduced to her. Mrs. Herldleen Russell would see that God wanted her life experiences to equip her and send her out to a world, hungry for Christ, thirsty for holiness, and yearning for the power of the Holy Ghost. In 1985, Mrs. Russell and her husband were conducting a revival in Yorkshire, England. Early that morning during her devotional time, the Lord spoke to her and said, *"Ask of me and I'll give you the heathen for an inheritance and the uppermost parts of the world as your possession,"* Psalm 2:8. So she was obedient to His request although she didn't know what to expect in the future.

Later, Sister Russell was the only African American invited to join women of AGLOW International travelling to Guatemala. (Aglow International is a Transformational Kingdom Culture with mindsets not of this world. A Kingdom Movement, it is committed to seeing God's will done on earth as it is in Heaven by raising up champions and warriors across the earth who will bring freedom to the oppressed while providing opportunities for everyone in its spheres of influence to grow into radiant relationships with each other, as well as, the Father, the Son, and the Holy Spirit.) Her first assignment was to teach men, and ministry to men later became her destiny. She spoke using two interpreters. Then she and the group went up into the mountains, where the people had never seen Americans. The next day, the group traveled on the back of a truck down to the beach. They ministered, taught, and prayed with Guatemalan women to receive the Baptism of the Holy Ghost. Next they went to Guyana, South America to conduct revivals. Sister Russell learned that COGIC women were also making a significant impact on the continent of Africa. She learned that Dr. Mallory was not a tourist but visited the continent with purpose and an appointment. She brought students from Liberia to the U.S. for educational opportunities. She knew that education was the key to success in this world. Sister Russell also learned of Missionary Lott, who dedicated her life to missions work and oftentimes wondered if they were related. Mother Coffey's objective for starting the National Women's Convention was for the purpose of raising funds for missions. She had traveled to Haiti to visit the work there and committed resources to supporting COGIC missionaries.

In 1992, Sister Russell was invited for her first trip to Nairobi, Kenya, Central Africa to conduct a women's retreat. She was excited to say the least. She had no entourage to accompany her, just great examples that went before her. Pan African Christian Women Association (PACWA) an international ministry was the invitee. When Sister Russell arrived, there were several hundred women assembled in a small college and after the ministry and teaching they sought to receive the Baptism of the Holy Ghost.

In 1997, the Lord spoke to Sister Russell and said that it was time to go back to Africa. That same year, she was invited to Uganda by a pastor to conduct a women's conference. While at this conference, a group of women traveled by bus from Kenya to ask her to conduct their women's conference. For the next three years, twice a year Sister Russell went back and forth to conduct the women's conferences in Uganda and Kenya. She witnessed such a strong faith and saw many come to Christ, receiving the Baptism of the Holy Ghost, and healings.

In 1999, the Youth of Uganda asked Sister Russell to be the keynote speaker at their RIOT (Righteous Invasion of Truth) Conference, in Jinja. She organized the first youth team to accompany her to exchange knowledge/culture and to teach holiness. It would be the beginning of the Youth teams, organized to go to Jinja, Uganda. It was at one of these conferences that a young lady received Christ as her Savior and her call to study medicine to become a physician. <u>Ten years later</u>, when Sister Russell took a team of women from the U.S. to host a Women's Health Initiative Conference, a team member became very ill. They had always prayed that this never happen because the health resources were inadequate. It became necessary to take the team member to a medical clinic. When the team member arrived there, the doctor that came to examine and treat her was that same young lady who had sat in the youth conference many years before. She had been praying for medical supplies for the clinic…and that year medical supplies were donated to the Dr. Herldleen Russell Ministries by a hospital in the U.S., some of which they were able to share with this Christian doctor. GOD IS JUST AWESOME!!!!!!!!!!

In 1999, after ministering and concluding one of her trips, The Lord again spoke to Sister Russell and said, "Ask for Africa." After a few protest questions…She said to Him, "Give me Africa." He quickly answered her and said, "It will not be what you think. You will teach and train pastors." When she came out of her room, a pastor was waiting to speak to Sister Russell and asked her if she would come and conduct a Pastor's Conference for the pastors there. She laughed…and said, "Do you know what the Lord spoke to me about 10 minutes ago?"

In 2000, the pastor's conferences were launched and Sister Russell took teams of pastors and missionaries skilled in ministries needed by these pastors. The Dr. Herldleen Russell Ministries hosted yearly conferences throughout Uganda, Kenya, and South Africa. The Lord, told her to take conferences to villages to pastors would never get opportunity to ever go to a conference. So many Africans said, the White brothers and sisters come but they wondered when our Black brothers and sisters would come and see about them.

Sister Russell was asked to start a COGIC church and with the permission of the late Bishop D.W. Spann and Bishop Moody, the first COGIC church was started. It was her tradition at the end of the conferences to sit and speak to the pastors of their needs. One 71 year old man, who pastored 70 churches, simply asked for a bike so that he could travel back and forth to his churches in the villages, his bike was worn out. Other pastors requested Pentecostal schools and expressed other needs. Sister Russell told them she could not supply these things but that she represented COGIC.

In 2003, at her request, Bishop Bobby Henderson accompanied Mother Russell and met with pastors and the Republic of Uganda COGIC Jurisdiction was formed. He appointed her as his Supervisor of Women. The convocations had far reaching results, the Jurisdiction numbered over 100 churches in Uganda and over 80 in Kenya. At the convocations the women requested their own time, thus the Women's Convention/Conference started. The first Women's Convention had over 3,000 women in attendance. Supervisor Russell would take a team of health professionals as well as teachers to host Women's Health Initiatives. Not only did they pray for AIDS inflicted women but they were able to teach them how to take care of themselves and their children. The Dr. Herldleen Russell Ministry annually took clothing and school supplies for the children to the conference.

In 2005, Pastors wanted more than an annual conference and they asked for a School of Ministry. By this time God had added educators, administrators, and teachers to the team. Supervisor Russell started the first School of Ministry for pastors. Over 200 pastors have graduated. The following is a testimony given during a graduation ceremony. A graduate said his pastor told him it was time for him to go and plant a church in a village where there was no church. He said, "I don't know how or what to do." Someone told him about the Dr. Herldleen Russell School of Ministry. He enrolled, graduated and said, "Now I am prepared." The ministry has two campuses in Western and Central Uganda. They are now in preparation to take the school from a certificate level to a diploma. The curriculum writer is Dr. June Rivers.

About 2002, the building program began. There was a request to build an orphanage because the AIDs epidemic had left so many orphans. Mother Russell with the assistance of others completed the first orphanage with donations from churches and individuals. The orphanage was named after Dr. Ada Marshall, a former supervisor, and was built next to the church. Supervisor Russell's dream was that every COGIC church would build an orphanage next to it because all of the churches have orphans. She calls the orphanages Hope Centers.

In 2012, the school in Mpigi, Uganda was completed with a primary school and later the Bishop Wooten extension was added. A YOAM team, led by Dr. June Rivers would join Supervisor Russell and her team later and train teachers, host activities for the children, and completely furnish the primary classrooms. A portion of the YOAM team headed by Chuck Rivers helped to build a church in Buyala.

In 2012, Pastor Boneface, who graduated from the School of Ministry, asked Dr. Russell would she come and host a Men, Women and Youth Conference in Ibanda, Uganda so that they could also gain some of the knowledge that he learned in the School of Ministry. The people in this remote village had never experienced a conference. Mother Russell discovered that Pastor Boneface was attempting to conduct a school in one room of his church because the children of his area were not going to school. The government school was too far and some children were being snatched by witch doctors on their way to school. He asked Dr. Russell and her team to help. In 2013, after prayer and receiving a plan, ground was broken for the Dr. Willie Mae Rivers Educational Complex with an adjoining Hope center whereby orphans would be in walking distance to the school. This complex will be six buildings when completed. Partnering with the Education Committee, Dr. Wilma Huey, Chair, Mother Rivers and The Department of Women, the classrooms have been completed where over 200 children were registered and attending. This project has been more extensive than the partners envisioned.

In June, 2015, June Rivers had the honor of attending the ribbon cutting of the Dr. Willie Mae Rivers' school where 1,000 people were in attendance including a member of Ugandan Presidential staff and numerous other government officials. This complex is a prototype for individuals to observe how a first class school should be built and operated in a village. The administrator of education will bring retired U.S. teachers to train the Ugandan teachers and teachers that would come from the adjoining villages. They will be taught techniques and strategies for teaching reading, mathematics, and science to take back to the various small village schools.

Yes, Dr. Mallory…education *is* the key and a quality Christian education is required because God's standard is never second best. Dr. Mallory's legacy continues in this remote village in Ibanda, Uganda. The school is open to all and will build future leaders in an under developed country. Government officials stand in awe at this accomplishment and are now pledging money to help and partnering with Dr. Herldleen Russell Ministries. The Hope Center, along with two more buildings in the complex will be completed by June 2016. The land has been purchased next to the Hope Center for the orphans to plant their own food and harvest it. Mother Russell is also supervising the building of a school financed by City of Refuge, Mt. Rose COGIC in Crosby Texas, pastored by Dr. Ron Eagleton.

Water4 is an organization that drills wells throughout Africa. *Water4* in partnership with the Oklahoma 3rd COGIC jurisdiction, Bishop Malcolm Colby and Deacon Walter Chandler (jurisdictional liaison), have sponsored wells for the school, the village, the church, and the orphanage. *Water4* is unique in that they train the villagers how to install wells which gives them job opportunities to go to other areas to drill and repair wells if broken. The endeavor of the partnership is to have a well for every COGIC church in Uganda. *Water4* also honored Dr. Russell as one of their 2015 ambassadors.

Future goals of the Dr. Herldleen Russell Ministries include agriculture and healthcare. Since farming is the Ugandan way of life, this ministry will partner with universities to bring agricultural students to teach them better farming methods. The medical arm of the ministry is now partnering with the medical community to build clinics and to partner with hospitals to provide medication for the clinics.

Supervisor Russell has learned that when the Lord gives vision, He gives provision and favor. He is a Phenomenal God that uses ordinary people. God faithfully ordered her steps so that she can fulfill His divine plan.

Emma Rose Sanders

The life of Supervisor Emma Rose Sanders is similar to that of the other women interviewed for this chapter. She was influenced by her mother, she formed partnerships outside COGIC, worked as a registered nurse to fund most of her ministry, and feared no man or Satan.

Emma Sanders was not born in a middle-class family but rather to a poor family in rural Mississippi, and was the eleventh child out of fifteen born to a Church Of God In Christ Evangelist missionary mom. Her father was absent from the family most of the time but her mother (91 years old and still a soldier at this writing) loved Jesus, loved people, and went about her community with her children doing missions work. Willie Bell Hayes was Emma's early example. Her mother was a resident beautician who raised the morale of those women who may not have had such a great self-image. Her Mother sewed clothes and gave them for free to those who were less fortunate and for those who could afford to pay a nominal charge. With that money she purchased more fabric. Her mom tells it like this, "I knew God had something special for Rose, the devil has tried to kill her since she was born, but each time and through each affliction God delivered. She has never let anything stop her." Mom says that there was no job ever too dirty, there was nobody ever too old or smelly that Emma was not willing to help. From washing baby diapers when she went to help a new mother, to emptying old people's pots, helping to kill chickens, and skinning animals at a young age.

Emma grew up on the dirt roads in Mississippi barefoot with outdoor toilets, no electricity even up until the early 60s. Although, there was a well in the yard there was no running water. Yet she grew up blessed according to Romans 8:28, "And we know that all things work together for good to them that love God, to them who are the called according to his

his purpose." Her past life experiences were in preparation for her present work, such as the haven where she grew up in and under the eagle eyes of her older sisters. Going to church and being exposed to Jesus, she accepted His gift of salvation at the ripe age of seven.

Being exposed to the Gospel Missions by living in a community where it was just normal to help everyone and protect everyone just kind of thrust her into caring and sharing what she had. As she watched and helped her mother make literally thousands of quilts given away to cover those who were cold or just to bless them; she watched as her mother shared what little food they had with people who were homeless. Sometimes total strangers came to stay with them. She never remembers a time when her mother was not working on some project for someone else. Yes, her mother preached but more than that her mother "practiced" practical missions. Emma was called from birth but the developmental process took a while. God was ordering her steps in preparation for her to fulfill God's divine plan.

It was Emma's dream to become a nurse. From the time she was a little girl she wanted to help old people, be a champion for those who could not speak for themselves, and make people well. She nursed animals and she nursed people. Two of her younger siblings died in infancy so that developed in her the hunger to help children. When she moved to Indianapolis, Indiana she expected great thing in that city. It was a shock for her to see that poverty existed to a greater extent in the city than in her rural Mississippi community. Emma's upbringing in Indianapolis saw a continuation of what she experienced in rural Mississippi. She continued to hang out with the elderly and to learn from them. She continued to help those who were less fortunate by building bicycles, learning to sew, visiting people, fixing things, and she never had problems navigating her way through diverse cultures. This is one of the reasons she feels that God was calling her even as a child to ministry.

She graduated from a vocational high school and learned some Spanish. It was not her desire to travel abroad but to impact the community where she lived. At that point she was already feeding the hungry and sewing for the less fortunate. A few weeks after she was married, the Lord told her that she would go to nursing school for the ministry that he would give to her and her husband. Her husband was not preaching at the time, he was only a good brother. She didn't have any money or any access. She and her husband were raising four children because his mother had passed away prior to their marriage. So Emma felt that it was her job to stay home and make sure that these children were raised while she balanced ministry as her mother had done. Before long, she started her own family. Her eyes were open and so was her heart for the community and the church. Always active in her church, she also steered several civic committees. Upon her discovery that there were hungry neighborhood children, she organized a feeding program that served meals three times per week. The program periodically gave clothing away. She used her home to sell and make clothes for the neighborhood children. She contributed to national missions never dreaming that God was preparing her for the same.

Mother Sanders knew that God was preparing her for foreign missions when the Church Of God In Christ, UNAC came to Indianapolis in the mid-90s. As part of the host jurisdiction she was very tired having organized a picnic and several receptions for the convention. Nevertheless, she attended a special mission's service. Sitting on the back row with her sister, with her cane near due to a condition that at times rendered her immobile, she listened. When Bishop Bobby Henderson made the altar call that day he said, "I'm not making this call for those who want to be saved, I'm making this call for missions' workers." Nobody went forward. So she said to her sister, "I feel God is telling me to go but I'm already so busy I have too much to do." By that time she had finished nursing school, she was working, she had children at home, and her husband was pastoring. But the 'unction' of the Holy Spirit was in her belly to get up and go to the altar. So her sister said, "If He is telling you to go, you better go."

Sister Sanders walked down that long aisle with her cane and was the first one at the altar. She thinks some others came up but Bishop Henderson came over to her and prayed. Then he said, "I'm not going to tell you where to work but the Holy Spirit is going to tell you in a few days what you are to do." Then he prayed again in tongues. Sister Sanders broke down and cried because even at the altar, she was telling God that she was too busy and she needed strength to do the things she was already doing. However she loved the Lord and she was committed to Him. A few days later, she was working on a project as the liaison between the *National Right to Life* and the Indiana Black community as the *Black Americans for Life* president. She got a call from someone at a local office and they said, "We need someone to speak for us and to represent us at a convention of Black Pro-Lifers in Texas. Are you Black? Could you go?" That is how Sister Sanders became the national spokesperson for *Black Americans for Life*. She was sent to Texas to meet with a group of like-minded Black individuals. She was instrumental in forming a group called

LEARN which stands for Life Education and Resources Network. It remains the premier group for the championing of Black life in the womb; this initiative catapulted her into the national spotlight. The training included everything from handling media presence, to speaking in sound bites, to multicultural training, to handling press conferences, and to speaking at major conferences. God was giving her free training.

In 1998, from this pre-born missions work, she met a presidential candidate of South Africa, Kenneth Meshoe, an Assemblies of God Pastor. He was insistent that she come to South Africa, to help with the campaign and to do some teaching as apartheid had just ended. Medical intervention training needed to be done in the township hospitals and clinics. She knew no one in South Africa. Not even the pastor whom she had just met. Every excuse, Emma offered for not going, the Lord removed. There was no answer except, yes. The money to go was handed to her. The projects that she was working on, someone else willingly completed. Her trip to South Africa was a 15 hour flight with turbulence that knocked everyone from their seats but she said to God, "You told me to come and here I am." She stepped off the plane not knowing who would meet her, but there was a little Dutch lady holding a sign that read her name. She stepped toward the sign and shook hands with Olga who said, "You will come home with me today." She went home with someone she had never seen and that was the beginning of her journey 'into the everywhere.' It was truly a multicultural experience. On that trip she stayed with the Dutch, the Whites, the Indians, the Coloreds, and the Blacks. She even stayed in a convent. She nursed AIDS babies, ministered in churches, spoke in schools, and was interviewed on radio and television.

She also ventured into the squatter camps on a daily basis where she observed much suffering. Her most painful memory was a day of ministry in one squatter camp where all the people were given only bread and bones. She was struck by the gratefulness of the people, so much gratitude for so little. At that moment, she repented of her reluctance to come and to minister on that continent. "I'm only one person," she said. "What can I do?" He pointed out to her at that moment that education was the key. So instead of giving individual monies or scholarships, she established a home which is still in existence for pregnant women. She established a relationship with the Church Of God In Christ Church in South Africa that she never knew existed. Sister Sanders' missions to that point had been outside of the Church Of God In Christ and had been purely educational and humanitarian in Haiti and in the Democratic Republic of Senegal. She went back to South Africa the following year to establish a sewing school, beauty school, and an ongoing feeding program which feeds only twice a week but it had to be more than monthly because people at that time were really suffering. The sewing school went on to get contracts for all the school uniforms in the area so they were quickly independent.

In 2000, Sister Sanders was at a missions service and she heard God say call June Rivers. She reasoned that the trip was too near and it was too late. Besides it was Africa and too hot. But the nudging would not stop so she found the number and called, asking about the trip to Liberia. She found that the group needed an electrician. Since she was a licensed electrician she told Sister Rivers that she would go and wire the church. This was the headquarters church in Monrovia, the capital, that had been bombed during the Civil War. Elder Havious Green had previously sent money to rebuild the walls and to put on a roof. The YOAM team put in a 3000 square foot cement floor, while Sister Sanders and another team member who was an engineer wired the entire church.

Sister Sanders suffered many trials on this trip. She lost her luggage, which was stolen in Ghana. All of her tools were lost. For seventeen days she was in Liberia without any fresh outer clothes. During the first week, God provided a private room for her that no one wanted at the mission compound. It needed cleaning and was bare, but God provided a stool and a broken down lawn chair for her to sit and sleep. It was a space for her with no clothes, to wash what she had each night and rise before everyone to retrieve them. That room soon became the prayer center for those seeking quiet. On that trip God connected her to a son that is with her until this day. The conditions were so terrible that she actually thought she would never ever go back. It wasn't the culture shock, it was a spiritual thing. She resolved to never go back but God had other plans.

Mother Sanders had previously established herself in Senegal. At that point and even now there is no Church Of God In Christ in Senegal. Her first work was among the Muslims. God has given her favor with governmental officials, Port authorities, and administrators. God has shown Himself mighty in many situations. She tells of going to Senegal with two young missionaries who had never been outside of the United States and being deplaned in the middle of the desert at night because the airline they were flying on went on strike. When the pilot, speaking in French, stated they would not be able to land in Senegal a riot broke out on the plane. The plane was shaking in midair! The two terrified missionaries rushed and took seats next to Mother Sanders and they prayed while the fighting was going on. When the plane landed in an undisclosed location, the luggage was unloaded in the sand. Someone came along only speaking in French and what was said to the nationals only created more chaos. Mother Sanders asked for someone to speak in English and the man told her that he could not speak English. Operating in the Spirit she challenged the man about needing someone to speak English and he said to her, "Give me a minute, Mom." He gave her three boarding passes and told her that the Americans would be boarded first on the 1956 relic featuring windows papered over and broken seats. On broken steps they entered the plane which had to be propped up. Mother Sanders never saw or heard the plane land. One of the missionaries dropped her boarding pass in the sand and it was pitch dark. Mother Sanders asked the Holy Spirit to help her find it while her team and the two White missionaries who were also on the flight that she has assumed responsibility for hurriedly boarded. She found the boarding pass and was not trampled as everyone in a panic ran to get on the plane. Security guards came out of nowhere with guns and yelled for the Americans to board. Mother Sanders watched as an irate woman having an altercation with the guards was knocked out by the gun of a security officer and at the same time the guards reaching for Mother Sanders took her by her jacket and her skirt and threw her up the steps into the planes' entrance. Mother Sanders and her team prayed that the plane could take off. The smiling steward in a white suit asked the passengers not to put anything in the overhead bins. Everyone was to strap themselves into their seat. When the plane finally took off all of the seats were rocking chairs and everything in the overhead bins fell out but God took them to Senegal.

They faced another problem which occurred due to their

arrival a day late. At the time cell phones were not common and they had no way to contact someone to pick them up. They had missed their connections with their host and didn't have any place to stay for the night. So when they arrived at the airport there was no one to meet them and the young missionaries asked, "What shall we do." Mother Sanders said, "We will just pray." They sat down and a few minutes later a soldier walked up to her and said, "Are you Mrs. Sanders." She replied, "Yes." He told to her that the captain said to wait for him and he would be along for her in a few minutes. Again God had made a way. From that point in Senegal she had a military escort. Truly, God orders your steps so that you can fulfill His divine plan.

Mother Sanders partnered with Muslims for her secular work. The mission in Senegal was to educate children and so she had favor with the government and established four schools. There was no difference made between Christian and Muslim children, they simply had to be an orphan or among the poorest of poor Street children who had to work to be able to sleep. For almost ten years Mother Sanders sponsored the educational program in Senegal along with a program in Liberia including twenty-five children in five schools for total of 125 children. She shipped supplies, clothes, food, and furnishings into the country for those children. The program was later dissolved due to the lack of funds. Some Muslim parents became Christians due to the care of their children. Also, the Muslim women wanted a God that would change their husbands into loving men who would not beat them, require them to work, or have another wife. They wanted a Christian husband. The Muslim women noted how the Christian men treated their wives along with Elder Sanders who accompanied his wife on one of the trips. Mother Sanders had never thought of Christian marriages as a way to win Muslim women to Christ.

Later Mother Sanders found a Christian Church by accident. She heard someone praying in French and followed the sound to an upper room behind a wall. After the prayer, the members prophesied to her about the Muslim man that had been assisting her for years. They also warned her of the coming demonic attacks through animals who were the gods of the people. The pastor of this Christian church contacted Dr. Bryant, a medical doctor and Youth With A Mission (YWAM) leader in Senegal. Dr. Bryant had not responded to Mother Sanders' letters from the U.S. because he was too busy and could not handle any more responsibility. However, he came and took her to a beautiful mission compound where it was not expensive to stay. A hoard of lizards, sent by demonic assignment, invaded her room. She rebuked them and opened the door for them to leave. After that she experienced a peaceful night of sleep.

Through a partnership with CAPRO Ministries, a Christian organization headquartered in Nigeria that ministers to Muslims, Mother Sanders established eighteen Pentecostal churches. CAPRO supports Muslims who become Christians and are ostracized from their family and community.

Mother Sanders related another story about a container she had shipped from the U.S. that was held up at the port. Her faith in God was strong because she believed God told her that she would get it that day since it was her last day in that location. The authorities were stalling in an effort to gain control of the container. She told them all including her Moslem escort and business partner that God said she was to get the container that day and they responded, "It won't be today." So she fell to the floor and said, "God, you told me today." They said to her to, "Get up." She responded, "I cannot because He told me today and I have to have an answer." From out of nowhere a man came dressed in a khaki tropical suit and said, "I will help you." The man went back in one office, came out, went into another office, and then came to her and said, "Let's go to the Port. All the while her business partner and the other authorities were saying, you're too late but the man said, "Let's go."

Mother Sanders with the man in her car, returned to port. When she arrived, the individual who could release the container had left but she showed the people his phone number and told them to call him. They were reluctant to call because they thought he would not return so she called and had someone else to speak to him in French. He said that he would be right there and not to charge her any money. He drove up in a large Black brand-new Mercedes and all the people marveled and said, "It must be her God because he never comes. He released the container to her and gave her a driver for the truck. It was God showing Himself mighty. The man who showed up in the khaki suit went with her to deliver the goods. He had completed all the paperwork necessary to get the container released and then directed them to a place for storage and distribution. Waiting until the distribution was well underway, Mother Sanders turned to pay him but he was gone. No one saw him leave, no one knew who he was, no one knew from where he came. She would not have gotten her container without him. God ordered her steps and made provision for her to fulfill His divine plan.

Mother Sanders was working in Senegal, Haiti, and the Dominican Republic so she certainly didn't want to work in

Liberia. In 2003 Bishop Amos Nyema and the late Brother Abraham Brown told her that God said for them to choose her as the Supervisor of Liberia. She thought it was a joke because she didn't tolerate heat well. She referred them to her husband expecting him to say that she was too busy. After all she was the pastor's wife, she was working in her local jurisdiction and district, she was a mother, and about that time a grandmother. Instead Elder Sanders, her husband said, "If the Lord says so I'm sure he will give her the strength and vision to do it." Since being in Liberia she has undertaken the revitalization of the COGIC major mission station and numerous other projects.

Mother Sanders elicited a call for help in the Ebola Crisis in the November 2014, issue of *The Whole Truth*. With the help of Presiding Bishop Charles E. Blake, over $120,000.00 worth of supplies including an ambulance were shipped to the national defense to aid in the fight against Ebola. Mother Sanders designed a hand washing system that was better than the commercial ones that were made. She was in Liberia during the month of January 2016 doing the work that God has called her to do. Her adopted son, who was now a government official provided her with military escort and took her to meet President Ellen Johnson Sirleaf. God faithfully orders our steps so that we will fulfill His divine plan.

Lee Etta Van Zandt

Mother Lee Etta Van Zandt not only was influenced by her mother but was personally influenced by Dr. Mallory. She formed partnerships outside of COGIC to experience the work of missions. She served as a national evangelist raising funds for her missions work. Years later Mother Van Zandt was called to work in Brazil for 20 years and is presently the Supervisor of Women for the Maryland Eastern Shore Ecclesiastical Jurisdiction. She graduated in 1960 from Saints Jr. College while Dr. Mallory was still the President. Her family had a long history with Saints. Her Mother Gladys Paige Jones attended Saints, as well as many relatives. Lee Etta's family was from Mississippi and later migrated to Ohio, where she was born and raised. While at Saints, Lee Etta sang with the Saints Choir and traveled to help raise money for the School. Mother Van Zandt reports that Dr Mallory visited Africa and brought several African youth back to the Saints among them the late Abraham Brown and his wife, Jessie Brown who became her lifelong friends.

While attending Saints, Lee Etta met future husband, Benjamin Van Zandt of Alton, Illinois. Their lives were shaped by being under the leadership of Dr. Mallory. Lee Etta had already been involved in missions prior to her arrival at Saints. She began her international missions work at the *age of twelve years* when Mother Dorothy Webster Exume, missionary to Haiti, took her to that country. Later she traveled with the late Pastor L. G. Maddox and the late Bishop Bennett to British Honduras, which is now Belize. Elder and Mother Van Zandt were also able to bring ten young people to the USA to further their education. Phyllis, one of the students, yet lives in Mansfield, Ohio where Mother Van Zandt was raised.

Lee Etta's experience at Saints gave her a greater love for missions and a desire to live a life of service and sacrifice. After her marriage in 1962 to Benjamin Van Zandt, he supported her missionary work. Evangelist Van Zandt began going to Canada and Mexico every summer, working with friends from the Assembly of God Missions. Their ministry included street evangelism, Prison Ministry, and visiting Nursing Homes. Mother Van Zandt feels that Dr. Mallory influenced her ministry of helping young men and women in every way that she could. She connected General Supervisor Coffey with Mrs. Mary McLeod Bethune, the founder of Bethune-Cookman College. Mrs. Bethune has embraced a life of holiness early in her life. Mrs. Bethune and Dr. Mallory were friends, because they both loved God and were committed to the education of others. Dr. Mallory in her relationship with Mother Coffey helped to change the COGIC Department of Women from self-sanctifying to sanctifying the world. Dr. Van Zandt organized a conference thirty years ago called, *Victory Over Wounds Inner Healing* to help hurting women and men. Hundreds of souls have been delivered and set free through this ministry.

In 1995, when Mother Van Zandt went to Brazil there were four COGIC churches, one in the Rio area and three in the Sao Paulo area. She began to help Overseer Samuel Moore work and organize the Department of Women. In 2000, she was appointed as the Supervisor of Women. For several years, she took her husband, Elder Van Zandt, who was an accomplished musician, and some young people who helped train the Music Department which changed the music for COGIC in Brazil. Her friend Dr. Fay Ellis Butler and others came and helped shape the ministries of COGIC Brazil. Pastor Havious Green of Detroit along with his daughters, Dr. June and Dr. Connie and son-in-love, Charles Rivers contributed much time and finances to the work there. Dr Esther Butler of Brooklyn N. Y. along with Dr. Nicky of Atlanta, Georgia, conducted the Medical Clinic for the Women's Department year after year.

Later, Supervisor Van Zandt trained Beatrice Burns Booker of Atlanta, Georgia, who became the first resident missionary. Missionary Booker would live for six months of the year in Brazil working and implementing the work of the Department of Women and any other work of the church. Mother Van Zandt formed a partnership with the Assembly of God orphanage. Also, she bought land and built a home for Unwed Mothers. She and Bishop Samuel Moore raised funds to build a five bedroom Missions house where the Saints could stay when they came to Brazil. All of this was inspired by the Lady who grew up in a middle class family, but was willing to suffer and sacrifice having traveled and ministered in 75 countries. She lives to please God by heeding His call to go into the everywhere. God faithfully orders our steps so that we can fulfill His divine plan.

Conclusion

The women chronicled in this chapter have given service and experienced sacrifice by going into the everywhere. These women had five factors in common. One was the influence of their mothers who modeled serving others. The second factor was the partnerships that they formed to carry out the work was diverse and as with Dr. Mallory they partnered with individuals both inside and outside of COGIC. The third factor was that they gave much of their income to finance their international ministry. The fourth factor was the lack of fear in traveling sometimes in dangerous situations and remote locations. Importantly, the fifth common factor was their strong desire to serve God no matter the consequence.

There are many others like these four who have given tremendous service and extreme sacrifice. Mother Mary Beth

Kennedy along with her husband and children lived in a remote Liberian village for years and served in numerous other countries. Missionary Dollie Bennett Milfort lived in Haiti for eighteen years as a medical missionary. Mother Claraetha Spencer, who is the Supervisor of Turk and Caicos Island, recently returned from working at a School for Autistic Children. There are many others but with a membership of a reported 6 million, there should be at least hundreds mission minded Church Of God In Christ women serving around the world. Anthea Butler states that, "The shift in focus from civically engaging the world through sanctified living to internal COGIC squabbles and internal status has eroded the power of women." This observation or criticism seems harsh and even embarrassing but it is true. This shift took place post-Dr. Mallory and Mother Coffey era. Even in the Women's International Convention souvenir journals post-Mother Coffey do not include the history of Mother Robinson and Mother Coffey, who both lived lives of service and sacrifice. Pictures of international missionaries and the countries in which they serve are no longer included. This oversight or lack of focus on what God has mandated us to do, grieves Him. One of my grandmother's favorite Scriptures was**,** "He that hath pity upon the poor lendeth unto the LORD; and that which he hath given will he pay him again," Proverbs 19:17.

Dr. Mallory could have lived a different life, perhaps of fame and fortune. Mothers Norfleet, Russell, Sanders, and Van Zandt could live a life of ease without the stress of raising funds and organizing trips abroad. Perhaps they would be millionaires by investing the funds used for ministry to people all over the world. They serve and sacrifice with dedication and passion. They never fear the challenges that they encounter. These "Iron Ladies" pray that a new generation of women will be inspired to rise up and go sanctify the place to which they have been called. These women are truly convinced that as God has ordered their steps to fulfill His divine plan, He will do the same for millions of COGIC sisters.

Thank you for giving to the Lord,
I am a life that was changed
Thank you for giving to the Lord,
I am so glad you gave.

Excerpt from Glimpses

International Council of Women

In 1959, she was among the "Women Leaders of the Free World who participated in the policy making programs of the International Council of Women at its Executive Board Meeting in Vienna, Austria.

In the International Council of Women, she held one of the highest offices, Vice Convener of the Educational Commission. Nominated to this office by the Canadian Council, she was elected in 1960, during the Triennial meeting in Istanbul, Turkey which she attended as a delegate of the National Council of Women of the United States.

Interest in Africa

In 1960, organized the "Friends of Liberian Youth," a volunteer group of American women-grew out of Dr. Mallory's interest in Liberia, West Coast Africa, during a six week's tour of this country, as one of the special guest of President William V.S. Tubman at his fourth Inaugural Celebration. Dr. Mallory studied the rural school system throughout the area and observed the need for special assistance to promising youth in that setting. Upon return to the United States, she launched "F L Y" as a program specializing in the provision of transportation to bring students from the rural areas of Liberia to America for advanced educational opportunities. The headquarters of this organization was in New York City.

One of the first Americans to visit Ghana after it attained Commonwealth status, Dr. Mallory was invited to return in 1961 to attend the Conference for African Women and Women of African De[s]cent.

In 1962, Dr. Mallory attended the Executive Board Meeting of the International Council of Women in Rome, Italy.

In February 1967 Dr. Mallory was selected as a member of the International Platform Association.

In January, 1972, Dr. Mallory was awarded the Degree of Doctor of Sacred Literature by Pillar of Fire College and Seminary in York, England.

Her biography appears in <u>Who's Who in American Education; Who's who in the Southwest; The International Dictionary of Notable Presidents</u> – published in London, England.

In January, 1967, Dr. Mallory's biography appeared in the <u>Royal Blue Book, Leaders of the English Speaking World,</u> London.

In 1972, her biography appeared in Who's Who of American Women, published by Marquis Who's Who, Inc., Chicago, Illinois; The World Who's Who of Women, published by Melrose Press Ltd., International Biographical Centre, Cambridge, England.

Her biography appeared in the World Who's Who of Women, published in Cambridge and London, England, 1973.

Dr. Mallory was the subject of a biographical sketch in Eve, a Scandinavian Periodical.

Chapter Six

Dr. Arenia Mallory **at Lane College, Jackson, Tennessee 1960**

ARENIA C. MALLORY:
An Example of Spiritual Prowess

Romanetha Stallworth

The Word of God is filled with examples of the labors of godly women.
Mother E.F. Barron Texas Northeast

The Leadership style of Dr. Arenia C. Mallory is reminiscent of King Jehoshaphat in 2 Chronicles chapter 20 as well as that of a Servant Leader. Servant Leadership requires the creation and implementation of vision, setting and accomplishing challenging goals, through prayer and faith. It elicits the cooperation of all, as well. Jehoshaphat based his confidence in God on four (4) principle truths.

1. God has power over all people and situations.
2. God has been faithful to His people in the past and present.
3. God's people are helpless without Him.
4. God's promises are a sure foundation for faith; His active presence among His people means deliverance and victory.

GOD HAS POWER OVER ALL PEOPLE AND SITUATIONS.

At some point in her life, Mazy Mallory determined that her daughter, Arenia, would be trained and have a career as a concert pianist. There were few female Black concert pianists in the early 1900s (after traveling to Europe and performing with the Berlin Philharmonic in 1931 Hazel Harrison headed the Tuskegee Institute's Piano Department before beginning a teaching career at Howard University in 1936.) The hand of God was at work in young Arenia's life. He knows our end from our beginning and as Arenia trained at the Whipple Academy of Music week after week and month after month, the discipline and skill she learned would one day serve as a spark to enlighten thousands of lives.

When Arenia left her well-to-do family in Jacksonville, Illinois to attend Simmons University in Louisville, Kentucky, little did she know that her life would change forever. Simmons College of Kentucky dates back to 1879 when the General Association of Colored Baptist in Kentucky opened the Kentucky Normal and Theological Institute. Known as State University in 1883, by 1921 the name had changed again to Simmons University.

Unfortunately, in researching historical material from 1918 to 1931, including scrapbooks, yearbooks from 1921-1922 the writer found only one 1928 unsigned degree.

It was now her desire and determination to become a Missionary to Africa but instead Arenia was persuaded instead to go to Lexington, Mississippi to assist Professor Courts in leading the denomination's fledgling school with a few students. At a time of disenfranchisement of Blacks, severe segregation, and abject poverty she said, *Yes* to God and *Yes* to Bishop Charles Harrison Mason, the founder of the Church Of God In Christ, Inc. Many would rise up one day and call her Blessed for doing what God called her to do. But first, He would use testing through overcoming crises without warning, hostility towards her and her assignment to show that the core strength of her faith would help her to reach her goals and discover what she was made of.

GOD HAS BEEN FAITHFUL TO HIS PEOPLE IN THE PAST AND PRESENT

Facing what seemed to be insurmountable odds as she observed children without clothing or food, hopelessness in the eyes of their parents and little means to provide education, what was she to do since education was a vital component of upward mobility? In fact, Joseph Addison stated, "Education is a companion no misfortune can depress, no crime can destroy, no enemy can alienate, no despotism can enslave, at home a friend, abroad an introduction: in solitude a solace, and in society an ornament. It chastens vice, it guides virtue, it gives at once grace and government to genius. Without it, what is man? A splendid slave, a reasoning savage."

Like her father in the gospel and mentor, "Dad" Mason, Dr. Mallory displayed a fundamental belief in the value of education not as a means but as an end itself. Charles Harrison Mason was born in the late 1860s to former slaves and sharecroppers Jerry and Eliza Mason. Mason himself did not receive an early formal education but learned to read and write. He was miraculously healed of tuberculosis and dedicated his life to the Lord as a teen. He was baptized by his brother Rev. I.S. Nelson and licensed as a Baptist Minister at the Mt. Gale Missionary Baptist Church in Preston, Arkansas. Ever pursuing knowledge, Mason enrolled in Arkansas Baptist College to prepare himself for ministry. However, not shunning education, he became dissatisfied with what he found to be liberal teaching and left the school. It was his reading the biography of the famous Black American Evangelist, Reverend Amanda Berry Smith that he came to learn and embrace the doctrine of sanctification. He later met another Baptist minister, Rev. Charles Price Jones, who shared his belief in sanctification and they formed the Church of God as a holiness church with Rev. C.P. Jones as overseer. The name was changed to Church Of God In Christ after Mason received the name while walking down a street in Little Rock, Arkansas.

In 1906, the Azusa Street Revival was well underway. It was at Azusa that Mason received the Baptism in the Holy Ghost with evidence of speaking in tongues. Mason gave an account of his Spirit Baptism in a deposition in the trial *Avant vs. Mason:*

> After a while my very soul began to cry to God just like a pump without a sucker, and after a while you catch the water and the man is strong, even physically, so, after a while my desire seemed to become intense within me, and every breath seemed to become heavier as I looked to God.

I...heard a sound just like the sound of wind, a great wind...like in the Pentecost...and I gave up to God, not resisting him; I determined not to resist him, and after a while I went through a crucifixion, and after I had gone through that I was completely empty, my mind was sweet, at rest; my flesh was sweet, at rest.

I sat there a while giving up to God. The anthem of Heaven seemed to rise then; I felt myself rising out of my seat, without any effort. I thought at first it was imagination; then I saw it wasn't imagination. Well when I was drawn to my feet there came a light in the room above the brightness of the light of God. When I opened my mouth to say "Glory to God," a flame touched my tongue and my English left me, and I said "Glory" and then my hands was moved by the power of the Spirit of God. He had complete control of me. Now when this was over I was filled with the presence of God. I didn't move a foot; I sat there just as I am sitting now; I knew everything going on; the people even talking in the room. I was looking at them just as I am looking at you. God didn't knock me out. I saw others that were knocked out. (Goodson: 2011)

As a result of disagreement over the doctrine of Holy Ghost Baptism with the sign of speaking in tongues, Jones and Mason parted and the Church Of God In Christ was reorganized in 1907 as a Holiness Pentecostal church. God was faithful to Bishop Mason and on his way back to Tennessee He conducted meetings where Black and Whites attended, were saved and filled with the Holy Ghost.

With the power of the Holy Ghost, the saints and their children would succeed! Bishop Mason was also practical and after observing Ms. Pinkey Duncan teaching students, he offered the basement of his St. Paul COGIC to be used as a classroom. By 1917, an Education Board was established and the school reorganized "for the education of its youth, under the influence and guidance of instructors and tutors who had either accepted holiness or were willing to serve in a school under the supervision of those of that faith." Professor James Court was selected to head the institution. During one of his visits North, Bishop Mason met Miss Arenia Conelia Mallory and invited her South to work at the school. Shortly after Mallory's arrival Professor Courts died and Arenia assumed leadership.

She may have experienced a sense of overwhelming challenge as seemingly innumerable obstacles faced her – toilets were quite a distance from the building, a hand pump and spring water were the water system; wood was cut from the trees; iron stoves were the heating system. Food was scarce; the classroom where seven grades were taught was poorly equipped. However, like, Jehoshaphat, Arenia Mallory had a strong belief that the same God who had been faithful in the past would continue to be faithful to His people. She understood that in times of crises or challenge many give up but like Jehoshaphat she would inquire of the Lord. Even though the school was severely underfunded, Mallory placed a heavy emphasis on the intangibles of vision, prayer and faith. She also believed in access and outreach. She knew that the battles of educating the children in this poverty stricken place, were not hers but the Lord's. Her strategy consisted of addressing the needs and inequities in the society. Indeed, she would have been called a drum major for justice. In a letter dated February 13, 1942 to Claude Barnett, President of the Associated Negro Press Mallory says, "I am unafraid and determined that I shall represent the forgotten, and down trodden, rural Negro, as long as God gives me breath. (Tucker: 2009)

God was faithful in allowing her to meet and gain favor with those who would help the school including saints in Mississippi and the Church Of God In Christ at large. She further saw the need to expose students to the outside world through cooperative and innovative partnerships. She made friends with some of the White merchants in Lexington who she would sometimes get credit for the things the school needed. A close friend and mentor was the Bethune-Cookman College Founder Mary McLeod Bethune, who also faced obstacles to her aspirations to lift Black students through education. Through her association with Bethune, Mallory entered corridors of power where her work at Saints was exposed. These opportunities made fundraising easier. After a bitter struggle, Mallory reported that students were able to have access to new textbooks.

Students participated in May Day Parades where thousands gathered in downtown Lexington. There were track teams and field meets. Students were disciplined and academic excellence was demanded so that by the end of their senior year they were proficient in the required curriculum consisting of English Literature, General Science, Elementary Algebra, French, Biology, Plane Geometry, Civics, Sociology, American and Medieval History, Chemistry, American Government, and Economic Geography.

GOD'S PEOPLE ARE HELPLESS WITHOUT HIM.

God's choice of any leader is predicated on time, purpose and need. He knew if the school was going to thrive, Arenia would lead the way. Like Jehoshaphat, Arenia was convinced that God has power over all people and situations. In the midst of his challenge Jehoshaphat said to God, "We have no power to face this…. We do not know what to do, but our eyes are upon you." Mallory also knew the school was helpless without God's absolute direction.

Sometimes the struggle for academic excellence in the midst of battles of low funding or unforeseen crises may have wearied or discouraged her. Most likely she did experience those times. Some of the young created a song telling of the leanness of the time–

> I am so tired of beans/Instead of fat, they make me lean/Beans for your breakfast/Beans for dinner/Beans for supper time/Boiled beans, baked beans Stewed beans, beans rain or shine/Never had ham, chicken or lamb/Strange don't you see/In all my life I was never so tired of beans beans beans!

Dire conditions notwithstanding, another strategy Mallory employed, like Jehoshaphat in 2 Chronicles 20:22-22, was audacious: God directed her to appoint singers of praise who went out before her. The choir led the way with students like Garie Charlene Carr-Wortham, born in Lexington, one of 13 children. Early in life while attending Saints Garie traveled, sang and accompanied on the piano as they toured and ministered to raise funds for the school. These student had to be fed physically, educationally and spiritually. They prayed, they fasted, they sang Negro spirituals and they kept the faith.

Mallory knew that in themselves they had little power to provide, but their eyes were upon God. She knew that God's active presence among His people means deliverance and victory.

GOD'S PROMISES: A SURE FOUNDATION FOR FAITH

Dr. Mallory wanted the best for her students. If she was going to raise Saints Industrial School from two frame building on stilts, with no sanitary facilities, no outside lights, hand pumped water, kerosene oil lamps, water heated in a large iron pots outside for baths, tin tubs and wash board for laundry, wood stove heater, and wood for heating the buildings cut from the woods by the young men; she had to believe and convince others that God's promises are a sure foundation for faith. The students were taught education and that they must keep their lives in tune with God. Not only did she fast and pray, she understood the reality that all the students and faculty as well must engage in praising, worshiping and giving God thanks. This was accomplished by each student engaging in mandatory daily prayer. But not just once a day. Students were steeped in the tradition of prayer before beginning their day at 6:00 a.m. Dr. William Dean taught at Saints from 1964-1974 and explained that before breakfast they prayed, before class they prayed, they participated in noon day prayers, at the end of the school day they had prayer. Tuesday night Worship Services, Wednesday Bible Study, and Friday night Worship Services were mandatory. On Sunday students attended the church founded by Bishop Mason in 1897, St. Paul COGIC. (St. Paul was initially a national church. After Bishop Mason turned the church over to Northern Mississippi, the pastors were the prolific preacher Elder O.S. Sheard, Elder Percy Dean, and currently Supt. William Dean.)

Seeing the need to upgrade and modernize the campus, Dr. Mallory led the students and faculty in prayer. Like the good king Jehoshaphat all of what Dr. Mallory accomplished was grounded in her faith in God and commitment to Him. Difficulty after difficulty, crisis after crisis Dr. Mallory remembered that power and might was in God's hand. And God honored the work of her hands.

Except from Glimpses

The following are some of the distinguished persons the students and faculty had the privilege to see and hear speak on Saints College and Academy Campus.

Mrs. Mary McLeod Bethune, Founder-President of Bethune-Cookman College. She served 14 years as the President of the National Council of Negro Women. Named by President Roosevelt as Director of the Division of Negro affairs of the National Youth Administration.

Ethel Waters, the famous Negro star known nationally and internationally in theater, radio, and television. She was married to Eddie Mallory, the brother of Dr. Mallory. Eddie Mallory was a celebrity in his own right. His own Band played and traveled with Ethel Waters. He and his band played for Saints students—and entertained the Citizens of the town of Lexington.

Dr. James Herbert White, President of Miss. Valley State College 1950-1971. The College is now Mississippi State University.

Dr. Oswald Bronson, Jr., B.S. Bethune Cookman College-B.D. Gamow Theological Seminary-PhD Northwestern University, Former President, Charles Harrison Mason Seminary, Atlanta, Ga., Present position President, Edward Water College.

Dr. S.N. Ferngild, M.A. Clark University-EdD. Boston University

Dr. Leonard Lovett, A.A. Saints Jr. College- M.A. – Ph.D. – Past President Charles Harrison Mason Theological Seminary, Atlanta, Ga.

Mrs. Gladys Bates, Editor, The Mississippi Education Journal – Assistant to the Exterior Secretary – Teacher's Association, Jackson, Mississippi.

Bishop J.E. Alexander, State Bishop of North Western Texas at one time, Midland, Texas.

Dr. Walter Washington, President of Alcorn University, Lorman, MS.

Dr. David C. Jones, Director Title I Programs – Assistant Superintendent of Holmes County Schools – Member, Board of Director of Education for Saints College and Academy.

Dr. L. Edward Mann, Vice Chancellor, Pillar of Fire College and Seminary.

The Honorable Robert G. Clark, Mississippi House of Representatives – Headmaster of Saints Academy, Lexington, Mississippi.

Mrs. Hazel Brannon Smith, Editor, Lexington Advertizer Paper, Lexington, Mississippi.

Dr. Dorothy B. Ferabee, a Nationally known medical doctor of Washington, D.C. She was impressed by the work Dr. Mallory had done. She joined her in Miss. in the summer and inoculated 15,000 Negro children against Small Pox and Typhoid – the first time the children from the Delta and rural area had had the inoculation. This service was rendered without charge.

Ms. Ida L. Jackson, Oakland, California. The first person of color to teach in the Oakland California Public Schools. She was born in Vicksburg, Miss. and completed her education in Berkley, California. She was pleased with Dr. Mallory's accomplishments at Saints school and desired to help. She impressed her sorority sisters, as she was the National Basilius of the AKA, to come and assist her in setting up a clinic in MS on Saints College and Academy campus for deprived children. Dr. Ferabee was one of her sisters who came. They gave time, medical instruments, and all other supplies necessary for a good clinic. Ms. Jackson played a vital role in establishing the library at Saints Academy.

Mr. Henry Young, Graduate Saints College – Professor of Philosophy and Theology at the C.H. Mason Theological Seminary, Atlanta, Ga. – Presently, Assistant President of the Bethune-Cookman College, Dayton Beach, Florida.

Dr. D. Manning White, Chairman of the Division of Journalism at Boston University.

Dr. Woodrow Hicks, President, Board of Education for the Church of God in Christ – Member, Board of Directors for Saints College and Academy. Chicago, Illinois.

Bishop J.O. Patterson, Sr., National Presiding Bishop of the Church of God in Christ, Memphis, Tennessee.

Bishop Samuel Crouch, a friend to Dr. Mallory and Saints College and Academy. Gave much financial support to the school.

Mrs. Fannie Cothran, Director Radio Station WXTN, Lexington, Miss.

Attorney J.O. Patterson, Jr. Member of the House of Legislature, Memphis, Tennessee – Tenn. State Senate – Memphis Board of Alderman.

Bishop F.D. Washington, one of the first High school graduates from Saints. He was one of the few students financially able to pay his way through school. His Father and Mother, our dear friends, helped to support other students who had financial problems. He is among the most distinguished, dynamic, and able preachers in the U.S. His first opportunity in speaking experience started at Saints school. Dr. Mallory gave him his first speech and the opportunity to speak on the Program with Harmonizers and on the Educational Program at the Convocation in Memphis, Tenn. He served many years as President of the Board of Directors for Saints College and Academy. He played a vital role in the development and the survival of Saints College and Academy.

Mrs. Earnestine Washington, not as a speaker, but she graced our platform with that magic voice with the Master's touch, and called the "Star Song Bird." She loved Dr. Mallory and she and Bishop Washington gave her that devotion and love like a real son and daughter.

Bishop T.D. Iglehart, Jurisdictional Bishop, Texas.

Evangelist Dorothy Webster Exume, Former Instructor at C.H. Mason Theological Seminary – Supervisor of school in Haiti – conducted Religious Emphasis Services several times at Saints Jr. College.

Mother E. Gamble, Old Pioneer – State Mother of Eastern Florida.

Dr. Mattie McGlothen, National Supervisor of Women of the Church of God in Christ.

The Honorable Governor William (Bill) Lowe Waller, Former Governor of Mississippi.

Lieutenant Governor–Evelyn Gandy–Director of Public Welfare–Commercial Home Maker, Hattiesburg, Mississippi.

Mr. William Dean, Elder and Pastor of Sallis Church of God in Christ, First Black Superintendent of Education of Holmes County, Miss.

Mrs. Bernice Spragg

Mrs. Corine Morrous

Wish we could call names and tell about all the Old Pioneers who loved Saints School and Dr. Mallory. We have to mention a few pioneers and friends.

Bishop Ranger	*Bishop Shipman*	*Bishop O.M. Kelly*
Bishop Barker	*Bishop Reeds*	*Bishop Crouch*
Bishop Bailey	*Bishop Kelsey*	*Bishop Robinson*
Bishop Jones	*Bishop O.T. Jones*	*Bishop Hamilton*
Bishop T. Davis	*Overseer Rice*	*Bishop Y. Wells*
Bishop Riley	*Bishop Butler, Sr.*	*Bishop Anderson*
Elder Wells	*Elder White*	*Elder Lylum*
Bishop Cohen, Sr.	*Elder Crass*	*Elder Kensley*
Elder Page	*Elder Jones*	*Elder Curry*
Elder Taylor	*Elder Patrick*	*Mr. Eugene Thompson*

Mr. Jonas Anderson	Mrs. Pluma R. Garnett	Mrs. Eva Archer
Ms. Rosa L. Hoover	Ms. Alma Washington	Ms. Esidore Saffold
Ms. Amelia Polk	Ms. Jeanetta Smith	Ms. Callie Greer
Ms. Mary Thurmon	Ms. Mattie L. Hodges	Ms. Ethell Hamilton
Ms. Luvonia Nalls	Ms. Mary Donaldson	Ms. Mary Carey
Ms. Ella M. Cooper	Ms. Blanche Cooper	Ms. Lillian Anderson
Ms. Deserie Pennington	Ms. Molly Clark	Mr. Willie Edward
Ms. Genous Cooper	Mother L. Robinson	Mother Gamble
Mother Baker	Mother Woods	Mother L. Coffey
Mother Payton		

There are those who [were] employed in the beginning of Dr. Mallory's Administration and know the struggle, suffering, hardships, good days and bad days. The load was heavy but there were those who cared and shared, worked and smiled without pay until she could take the signing group out and raise some money. The salary range was $15.00, $20.00, $30.00, and $35.00 month. She taught us the spirit of giving our best regardless and having faith in God.

Chapter 7

Dr. Mallory's Tombstone, Illinois 1977

OUTLASTING LIFE

[H]elp Saints to continue to grow; then my service (and service of others) these fifty years will not be in vain. Dr .Arenia Conelia Mallory

We must keep in mind that the Church Of God In Christ experience is a part of the American experience. The church has taken the message of Pentecost across America and then into the everywhere beginning in the early 20th century. And Dr. Arenia Conelia Mallory engaged in intense educational evangelism to play a vital role in embedding its message into the fabric of the nation. She also lifted the stigma of inferiority among her students as she drilled into their psyche that they must *Walk in Dignity, Talk with Dignity and Live in Dignity.*

The famous inventor and educator Booker T. Washington is quoted as saying *"The greatest use of life is to spend it for something that will outlast it."* Dr. Mallory became a game changer when she made the decision to spend her life laboring for a great vision. Deeply embedded within the fabric of American society and the Church Of God In Christ today, are males and females who have gone on to serve as pastors, educators, titans of commerce, supervisors and others. She would view with satisfaction former students who continue her legacy of holiness and sanctification such as one of the most prominent alumni today, Jurisdictional Bishop Jack Whitehead, who also serves in key areas of national leadership in the church she loved and sacrificed so much for.

Prior to the death of Dr. Mallory in 1977, a Founder's Day Celebration was organized in her honor. College Presidents, educators, and former students joined Congresspersons, bankers, business owners and others to applaud her triumph in realizing her dream of a better life for the people of Holmes County, Mississippi. Despite obstacles Mallory firmly believed that as they sent out students equipped spiritually, morally and educationally to *Walk in Dignity, Talk With Dignity and Live in Dignity* those individuals would impact the nation and the world. Following are excerpts from testimonials on Founder's Day, April 1974. (To view original letters visit USC Digital Library, Center for African American Church History & Research Inc. collection at http://digitallibrary.usc.edu.)

Walter Washington, President, Alcorn A. and M. College, Lorman, Mississippi I have drawn from your strength since childhood...[when] I watched you as you drew strength from the late Mrs. Mary McLeod Bethune, who was your ideal and in whose tradition you still carry on. All of us in Mississippi are richer because you founded Saints College.

George Owens, President, Tougaloo College, Tougaloo, MS

John A. Peoples, Jr. President, Jackson State College, Jackson Mississippi [Y]our achievements and contributions have been an example for all educators in Mississippi to emulate.

David H. Wicks, Mississippi Valley State College, Department of Social Science, Itta Bena, Mississippi: Probably yours has been a long and thankless job at times, for you had to fight and survive in an arena which has been historically reserved for men. Your record of contributions and achievements is laudable indeed, and your place as a giant among American educators is secure and has been for some time.

Laurence C. Jones, Principal, The Piney Woods County Life School, Piney Woods, Mississippi

C.J. Duckworth, Executive Director, Mississippi Teachers Association, Jackson, MS: The honor being bestowed upon you today is far less than that you have given to this country…I believe, in fact I know, Lexington, Holmes County and America are grateful for God's gift of you. It has taken noble men and women to hold this planet together. You are unquestionably one of those women.

Cleopatra D. Thompson, Dean, Jackson State College

Lillian T. Towell, Downtown Senior High School, San Francisco Unified School District: As I review my accomplishments, educationally, socially and spiritually, I am more than confident that what I am together with what I am doing today stem from a set of values and goals derived from your motherly guidance and leadership while attending school at Saints College.

Sam Carter, CPI Associates Washington DC and Dallas, TX

Louise Maxienne Dargans, Director of Research, Congress of the United States, House of Representatives, Washington, D.C.: You have done so much good. You have made the world such a grander place with your presence.

Marion Beaver, Danville, Kentucky

Francine Reese Morrison, God's Ambassador of Song, God's Worldwide Music Ministry, Inc., Fort Worth, Texas: Time nor tongue, nor pen can express my appreciation to this great woman of God, who is destined as a legacy of our nation!!!

Kivie Kaplan, Chestnut Hill, Massachusetts

Irene Powell, Formerly of Saints College, Atlanta, Georgia

Marguerite Walton, Saints College, Lexington, Mississippi

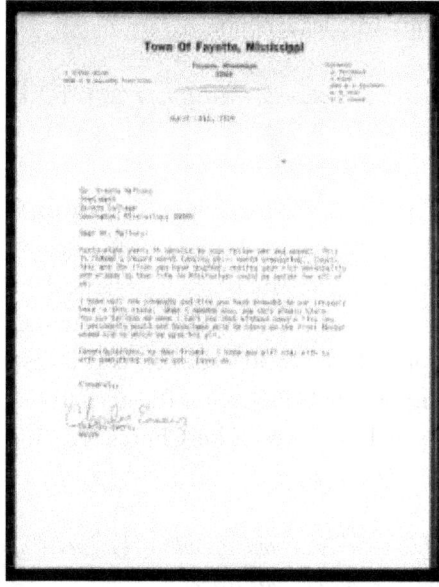

The letter above from Charles Evers, Mayor, Town of Fayette, Mississippi reads in part "I know well the strength and fire you have brought to our struggle here in this State. When I needed you, you were always there. You can believe me when I tell you that without people like you I personally would not have been able to carry on the fight Medgar waged and to which he gave his life."

Mrs. C. Collins Harvey, President, Collins Funder Home, Inc., Jackson, Mississippi

Dr. Woodrow W. Hicks, President National Board of Education, Church of God in Christ, International Headquarters, Memphis, Tennessee: Dr. Arenia C. Mallory…is certainly a woman of much vision. The foundation of her vision is embedded with great sacrifices for others, projecting beams of prayer to God in complete submission to His will, which personify true leadership.

Willie Mae Taylor, McComb, Mississippi MTA-NEA Council on Human Relations

Rev. Roy L.H. Winbush, Presiding, Church of God in Christ Publishing Board, Lafayette, Louisiana: We deem you a woman of great renown, a contemporary of Mary McLeod Bethune, Eleanor Roosevelt, and others who have attained to the halls of fame. As one of the world's greatest educators, thousands of lives of young people have been influenced and illuminated by your professional guidance. The Church of God in Christ is proud of you, Dr. Mallory.

W.R. Ellis, Jr., Chairman and President, Holmes County Bank and Trust Company, Lexington, Mississippi

Mother Becks: You have done a good job.

Attorney Calvin King, Durant, Mississippi

Members of the Holmes County Board of Supervisors, Lexington, Mississippi: We would also like to express our own personal appreciation for your many years of tireless work in helping to build and inspire the building of Saints from a tiny school in Lexington to an educational institution that has exerted a wide influence for good over much of our State and nation.

W.D. Wilson, Executive Vice President and Trust Officer, Holmes County Bank and Trust Company, Lexington, Mississippi

Holmes County School District, Lexington, Mississippi: As your associates on the Holmes County Board of Education, we are also aware of the many outstanding contributions that you have made to the public schools of this county. We especially appreciate your dedication to the proposition that all people need to be educated; that our schools ought to be updated in all areas; that high moral standards should be maintained by both students and teachers; and that Board members should have the courage to speak out and stand up for those things which will promote the best interest of the school children. (Editor's note: Dr. Mallory was a member of the Board, District 1)

N.C. Hathorn, Superintendent, Holmes County School District, Lexington, Mississippi

J.W. Moses, Mayor, City of Lexington, Mississippi: Your accomplishments in education, religion and your leadership will never be forgotten.

Fanny Cothran, Holmes County Broadcasting Company, Lexington, Mississippi

D. Marie Simmons, Saints College, Lexington, Mississippi: [Y]ou gave up your proposed life's career, and came to Mississippi to build an Institution for underprivileged boys and girls. Certainly, your love goes deep for humanity, or you would [not] have remained in this benighted area and suffered the obstacles that came your way….You have touched the lives of people nationally and internationally.

William H. Robinson, Saints, College, Lexington, Mississippi

E.M. Lashley, Saints College, Lexington, Mississippi: In many parts of the world, you have lighted the way for thousands groping in darkness mentally, spiritually, and morally. I am remembering when you told me your dream to help the underprivileged, the deprived, the poor, the needy people in Mississippi. Step by step, you have become the powerful and fearless person God intended for you to be, also showing the greatest test of courage bearing defeat without losing heart, yet, in spite of tribulations, sorrow, misfortunate, obstacle, unsympathetic, disinterested people of your own faith, (I was there) you kept the faith.

The following are a few names of Dr. Mallory's "children" and their achievements. The first six students are from one family of Lexington, Mississippi.

Chalmers Archer
Saints Jr. College, degree 1969 – Tuskegee Institute
BS and MS degree – Auburn University
Doctor's degree – Tuskegee Institute

Assistant Professor, Assistant to the Vice President, Tuskegee Institute, T. Ala.

Hermon A. Archer
Saints Academy, Diploma 1959
Howard University, BS degree
Employed, Department of Commerce, Washington, D.C.

Francis P. Archer
Saints Academy, Diploma 1951
Howard University, Washington D.C.
Employed, U.S. Post Office, Washington, D.C.

Evelyn D. Archer Rand
Saints Academy 1953
Howard University, Washington, D.C.
Employed, Bell Telephone, Washington, D.C.

Ansely J. Archer
Saints Academy Diploma 1957
Howard University
Presently at home with father who is ill

Vernon D. Archer
Saints Academy Diploma 1959
BS, MS, Howard University, Washington, D.C.
PhD Indiana University, Bloomington
Assistant Professor of Biology, Rutgers University New Jersey

Lillian Treadwell Powell
High School Diploma Saints Academy
BA, Dillard University, New Orleans, LA
MS, San Francisco University, San Francisco. CA
PhD Equivalent – Associate Professor in Education-Counseling at the University of California
Administrator in the largest high school in San Francisco, Calif
One of the first Harmonizers of Saints High School

Ruth T. White
Saints Academy Diploma
BA, MS San Francisco State University
PhD Equivalent
One of the first Harmonizers of Saints High School
Coordinator of Programs, Unison Elementary School, Oakland, CA

Rebecca McCain Champion
Saints Academy Diploma
Saint James Hospital, Director of Physical Therapy
Member, Board of Directors

Watkin Steele
Saints Academy Diploma
Owner of a very successful Real Estate Co., Detroit, MI

Clyde Smith
Saints Academy Diploma
Electrical Engineer, Space Program, New Orleans, LA

Dorothy Pearson
Saints Academy Diploma
Associate Dean of Social Work, Howard University, Washington, D.C.

Sandy Dixon
Saints Academy Diploma
MS, PhD Wayne State University
Business Administrator, University of Detroit, Michigan

Iris Miller Price
Saints Academy Diploma
Saints Jr. College, AA Degree
BS, Lincoln University
Teacher, Lexington Elementary School, Lexington, MS

THE JUBILEE HARMONIZERS

The Jubilee Harmonizers were the first all-female gospel group in the United States. Others were all male or mixed groups. Her faith in God with her prayer life and that dynamic personality carried her to the White House with a group of dedicated young girls from the cotton fields of Mississippi and Alabama to sing for President and Mrs. Franklin D. Roosevelt; Sarah Campbell Carroll, Allie Steel Crutcher, Laura Vaughn, Lillian Kiah, Lillian Tredwell Powell, Ruth Tredwell White, Mamie Miller, Makie Williams, and Miss Ella Mae Lashley, the Director.

Dr. Mallory found Sarah on one of the cotton fields of Alabama during a speaking engagement at one of the churches. She was almost blinded from picking cotton in the blazing sun and from severe sun strokes. Dr. Mallory could not forget this young woman's face and story. Only a few days passed before she with a friend returned to the plantation and brought Sarah, her Mother, two brothers, one sister, and one niece back to the school. Sarah traveled with the Harmonizers, crossed the continent several times, graduated, married and has three lovely children – two college graduates, one high school.

Allie Steel Crutcher graduated and is now the Supervisor for Provinces of Canada. Laura Vaughn is the Director one of the outstanding Brooklyn choirs and works for the Board of Education. Lillian Kiah lives in Cleveland, Ohio, married has a lovely family.

This final excerpt from *The Life of a Great Mississippian* tells of the passing of Arenia Conelia Mallory, this great American Classic into the Church Triumphant.

E.M. Lashley

The passing of Dr. Mallory sadden[ed] many hearts. One could not even attempt to measure the loss of her. The power of words could not express it. Her passing leaves an emptiness that can never be filled. We can rejoice and be thankful to God for having had the good fortune of being blessed by such remarkable human. She was called upon by the people in the community both white and black, by her children, and by friends far and near for advice.

If God calls you to a special task, He equips you and then helps you to do it. God gave Dr. Mallory the courage, faith, fortitude, and the perseverance to go knock on doors for He said seek and you shall find, knock and the door will be open to you. She began knocking and asking and God opened doors. The largest radio stations in some of the largest cities; KNOX St. Louis, WLS Chicago, etc. WXU Cleveland, Ohio gave her a thirteen-week' contract and that was quite an accomplishment, in light of those days and time.

Dr. Mallory is eternally loved by those pioneer employees of Saints school who yet lives, for she gave them something to be proud of:

Ms. Eula V. Simms	Ms. Cole Barker	Ms. Dovie Simmons
Mr. James Randle	Ms. Victory Jennys	Johnson
Mr. Frederick Bradley	Ms. Pastelle Redmond	Ms. Rozella Johnson
Ms. Ella Mae Lashley	Mr. George Austin	Ms. Olivia L. Martin
Ms. Elizabeth Lewis	Ms. Irene Powell	Ms. Eva Archer

Ms. Marguerite Cooper Walton	*Ms. Alma Eastmon*	*Ms. Elsie Shaw*
Ms. Elsie Washington Mason	*Ms. Eunice White*	*Mr. J.R Davis*
Ms. Suanne Evans Bronson	*Ms. Julia Callendar*	*Ms. Bobbie Wicks*
Ms. Consuella Carter	*Mr. David H. Wicks*	*Mr. Bennie Cooper*
Ms. A.A. Johnson	*Ms. Phoebe Donaldson*	

Contributors

Dr. Arenia Mallory was a giant of a woman physically (she stood over 6 feet tall) and educationally. The women who readily volunteered to present a portion of her story to a 21st audience are themselves full of good works. This final section is dedicated to learning more about them.

Cynthia Barbara Bragg is the daughter of the late Reverend Robert and Gladys L. Bragg. She graduated from Rahway Senior High school, obtained a B.S. degree from Morgan State University in Baltimore, Maryland, a M.R.E. degree from the Interdenominational Theological Center in Atlanta, Georgia, a M.S. degree from Iowa State University in Ames, Iowa and a PhD degree from American University in Washington, D,C. with a concentration in gender and a minor in the sociology of religion

Growing up in a closely knit family the "Bragg children" formed a singing group called the Bragg Singers—Lester, Alvin, Willie, and Cynthia. This was the "choir" for the founding church when their father, Pastor Robert L. Bragg was called by God to establish a church in Rahway, New Jersey. They were among the first/founding members of Holy Mountain Church Of God In Christ.

Dr. Bragg taught in the public school system at the junior and senior high school levels in Rahway and Piscataway, New Jersey for several years before moving from New Jersey to pursue a career in education. Little did she know at that time she would eventually serve in ministries (music and prison) and on boards (Missionary and Trustee Board) of her local church in Rahway. Her call to the missionary field motivated her to subsequently pursue theological study at the Charles Harrison Mason Seminary in Atlanta.

Currently, Dr. Bragg is Assistant Professor in the Department of Sociology & Anthropology at Morgan State University. She has presented papers at the American Sociological Association (ASA), the Society for Pentecostal Studies, (SPS), International Conference on Gender and Social Transformation, Beijing, China, and the First International Sociological Association Forum of Sociology, Barcelona, Spain. Dr. Bragg has also presented her research on women in ministry at Virginia State University, Petersburg, Virginia and at the 107th Holy Convocation of the Church Of God In Christ, St. Louis. More recently, Dr. Bragg was selected as a fellow at Princeton Theological Seminary in Princeton, New Jersey.

Dr. Bragg's involvement in ministries of the church, academic pursuits and current research on women and leadership in the Black church continue to enrich her life. Teaching is one of the mission fields she wholeheartedly works in and feels called to labor in this vineyard.

Dr. Willie A. Bragg is Assistant Dean for the School of Graduate Studies and Director of The Center for Continuing and Professional Studies at Morgan State University (MSU). Dr. Bragg received her B.S. degree from MSU in Elementary Education, a M.A. in Education/Early Childhood Education from Fisk University, and a Ph.D. in Special Education from Indiana University, Bloomington, Indiana. She completed a Post-doctoral Fellowship on Exceptional Programs for Culturally and Linguistically Diverse Children and Youth with Disabilities at the University of California, Santa Barbara.

Dr. Bragg's activities at Morgan State include, but are not limited to, directing grants and contracts, serving as liaison for MSU's collaboration with the University of Baltimore School of Law and leading efforts to develop an international partnership with William V.S. Tubman University, Liberia, resulting in a Memorandum of Understanding (MOU) between Morgan State and Tubman University. Dr. Bragg has also been instrumental in establishing collaborations with professional groups such as the Darlene H.

Young Leadership Academy, a professional development program under Blacks in Government designed to enhance leadership skills of government employees across the country.

In 2011, Dr. Bragg was successful in securing a $1 million dollar endowment from the Bernard Osher Foundation to fund the Osher Re-entry Scholarship Program, a program for nontraditional adult students enrolled in undergraduate degree programs at MSU. Since the inception of the program, adult recipients of Bernard Osher scholarships have graduated with bachelor degrees from the university.

Dr. Bragg has over 25 years of experience in higher education administration. She has taught and created courses (i.e., graduate/undergraduate) in early childhood and special education as well as facilitated workshops for regular and special educators during her tenure at the University of Cincinnati, Cincinnati, Ohio and Virginia Union University, Richmond, Virginia.

While at Virginia Union University, Dr. Bragg was selected by the governor to serve as a member of the Virginia Interagency Coordinating Council, a council designed to address issues related to families of young children with disabilities. She also authored and received grants from federal agencies and foundations focused on teacher preparation and early childhood education, curriculum design and evaluation, and university-community partnerships/alliances in higher education. Federally funded grants include several awards from the U.S. Department of Education, U.S. Department of Housing and Urban Development (HUD), National Institute on Disability and Rehabilitation Research (NIDRR), and National Institutes of Health (NIH).

Dr. Bragg continues to present at international, national, and regional conferences and holds memberships in several professional organizations. She currently serves as education consultant at her home church, Holy Mountain, Church Of God In Christ, Rahway, New Jersey, Founder, the late Reverend Robert L. Bragg and Co-founder, the late Missionary Gladys L. Bragg.

A native of Los Angeles, Mother Barbara McCoo Lewis was baptized in the Holy Ghost at the age of nine and is a third generation member of the Church Of God In Christ. Married to Bishop James A. Lewis since 1962 they are the proud parents of Elder James A. Lewis Jr and Supt. Jeffrey M. Lewis (wife Floetta) who is now senior pastor of the New Antioch Church Of God In Christ co-founded in their living room by Bishop and Mother Lewis in 1970. Her pride and joy are her adult grandchildren Shannon and Jeffrey Jr.

She has served in administrative, teaching and leadership capacities from the inception of New Antioch and is presently the Prayer and Bible Band President/Teacher. Her community efforts have earned her recognition by the Mayor for her extensive outreach work in Juvenile Halls, Street Ministry and Drug Rehabilitation Centers. Local Los Angeles newspapers honored her as "woman of the year" and the First Ladies Community Impact award. Mother Lewis, selected in May 1988 by Jurisdictional Prelate Bishop Charles E. Blake to serve as the Jurisdictional Supervisor, received her National Department of Women appointment November 1988 from General Supervisor Dr. Mattie McGlothen. Bishop Joe L. Ealy is currently her Jurisdictional Prelate.

Like Dr. Mallory, who was one of her mentors, Dr. Lewis is an innovator with many programs implemented over the past twenty-six years. Among the most significant accomplishments is the completion in March 2002 of the $4.7 million dollar 41-unit Hale Morris Lewis Senior Complex, the focal point of community distribution of food, clothing, toys, and health/hygiene products. Weekly Bible studies, computer classes, quarterly health-screening and senior awareness workshops are all part of life-enhancing services.

A servant-leader, Mother Lewis maintains communication with the women through four weekly prayer lines which target different categories of the constituency of women. Not only a renowned prayer warrior she is an anointed writer and has authored "The Christian Woman's Guide to Church Protocol and Saintly Decorum." She was the managing editor of curriculum guides and handbooks for the Jurisdictional School of Licensing for Missionaries, Regional/District Missionaries, Aspiring, Deaconess and Evangelist Missionaries, Clergy Wives, Auxiliary & Unit Leaders.

Her educational achievements include: Associate of Arts, West Los Angeles Community College; BA in Journalism, California State University at Los Angeles and Master of Arts in Theology, Fuller Theological Seminary. She was honored with a Litterum Doctorate degree from Southern California School of Ministry.

She serves on the national level as a member of the Presiding Bishop's Senior Executive Planning Commission. In April 2013 she was elevated by the Presiding Bishop to Assistant General Supervisor and Chairperson of Executive Business Affairs for the Department of Women under the leadership of the General Supervisor Mother Willie Mae Rivers. She is a member of the Executive Board, International Marshal, Program Committee Chairperson and Chairperson of the Special Convention Assistance Committee. Mother Lewis also serves on the Board of Trustees, C H Mason Theological Seminary in Atlanta, GA. The theme of her life is "I can do all things through Christ which strengthens me."

The Church Of God In Christ has churches in over 80 countries and since her 1989 appointment as Youth on a Mission (YOAM) leader, it has been the responsibility of Dr. June Rivers to take a team of adults and youth to a different country each summer for two weeks. Together June, husband Chuck and her daughter, Carla (since age 11 months old) have been an integral part of short term missions trips to Argentina, Bahamas, Barbados, Belize, Brazil, Chile, Costa Rica, Cuba, Dominican Republic, Guyana, India, Jamaica, Liberia, Malawi, Mexico, Nigeria, North Dakota, Panama, Philippines, South Africa, Trinidad, Turks and Caicos Island, and Uganda. She has traveled to over twenty countries since 1989, sharing the liberating power of the gospel in a spirit of excellence. She has been to several of the countries multiple times. Like Dr. Mallory, she shares an insight to impact the global community. Dr. Rivers challenges 21st century leaders to have a vision to impact the future.

Dr. Rivers retired as an educator from the Detroit Public Schools after 35 years and has also taught undergraduate and graduate level reading courses as a graduate assistant and as an extension lecturer for Michigan State University. She earned undergraduate and graduate degrees from Wayne State University. She earned a Masters of Divinity Degree in Counseling in 2013 from Ashland Theological Seminary and a Ph.D. from Michigan State University.

June Rivers is a member of Antioch Church Of God In Christ, Detroit, Michigan. She teaches Sunday School, tutors students in reading weekly, and is the director of Vacation Bible School. From 1991 until 1993, June was the writer for the *Primary Student*, Vacation Bible School materials published by Urban Ministries, Inc., Chicago. She is the author of "The Great Commission's Impact on a Short-term Missionary and Lay Leader in the Church of God in Christ," *Teaching All Nations Interrogating the Matthean Great Commission*, editors Mitzi J. Smith and Jayachitra Lalitha, Minneapolis, MN: Fortress Press, 2014.

Sis Rivers' greatest joy in life is to teach children about Jesus and how to be successful in school. She has years of experience teaching teachers and children about the elements necessary for becoming a proficient reader. Also, she loves mentoring parents to help their children reach their fullest potential. Her present personal goal is to develop an intimate prayer life in order to glorify God and to listen for His voice about the future direction of her life.

Supervisor Romanetha Stallworth is a woman who knows God and is known of Him. She has served as an Evangelist Missionary for 38 years and has traveled the United States and foreign countries to tell others about the saving power of Jesus Christ. Evangelist Missionary Stallworth was appointed Jurisdictional Supervisor of Women, December 2010, by

Bishop Dwight Haygood, Sr., Prelate of Kentucky First Jurisdiction.

Through the leadership of General Supervisor Willie Mae Rivers, the Lord used Supervisor Stallworth to bring the word of God during the 2003 National Women's Convention in Tampa, Florida. In 2004 she was appointed National Evangelist. In 2006, 2007 and 2009 she presented in the WIC Symposiums. In 2007 she served as Local Co-chair of the National AIM Convention. She was selected in November 2010 and 2016 to be the keynote speaker at the National YWCC Breakfast in the Holy Convocation.

Her education includes a bachelor's degree from University of Arkansas at Pine Bluff and a Masters of Education in Educational Psychology (Marriage and Family Counseling). She currently is in private practice as a Marriage and Family Counselor.

Supervisor Stallworth continues to experience the power of God. She has been healed from a stroke, cancer and heart disease. She is a walking testimony of a yielded vessel and God continues to use her in these last days to assist others in their walk with God. Her greatest testimony is that she is Saved, Sanctified and Filled with the precious gift of the Holy Ghost!

Selected Bibliography and References

Academy of Political Science.
https://www.psqonline.org/AboutAPS.cfm

Anderson, J. (2016, March 2). *Proposals Perpetuate unequal treatment to select UNC schools.* Retrieved from http://wilmingtonjournal.com/proposals-perpetuate-unequal-treatment-of-Select-unc-schools/

Bragg, Cynthia. 1992. *"The Church of God in Christ: A Religious Institution in Transition."* Master's Thesis, Department of Sociology, Iowa State University, Ames, Iowa.

Brown, Mayme Osby. "*Mississippi Mud.*" The Crisis, May 1936, 142. *This article perhaps ran in a series of articles in the black press of the 1940's and 1950's on Mallory. It was included in the Claude Barnett Papers, the founder of the Associated Negro Press wire service for African American newspapers*

Burns, Calvin.1990. *"Bishop Ford Directs Saints to Old Landmark: New COGIC Prelate Heads First Convention."* Tri-State Defender, November 10-14 1990, pp.B1

Butler, Anthea D. *Women in the Church of God in Christ: Making a Sanctified World.* Chapel Hill: University of North Carolina Press, 2007. ISBN 987-0-8078-5808-0.

Butrymowicz, S. (2014, June 27). *Historically black colleges are becoming more white.*

Carter, J. (2016, January 26*). Five signs a State is trying to close merge, an HBCU.* Retrieved from http://hbcudigest.com/digest-five-signs-a-state-is-trying-to-merge-close-an-hbcu/
Retrieved from http://time.com/2907332/historically *black-colleges-increasing-serve-white-Students/*

Davis-Adeshate, J. (2014). Dr. Arenia Conelia Mallory Foundation. Retrieved from http://www.dracmallory.org/

Davis, J. (2009). *Black just like my mama.* CreateSpace.Amazon.com

Digitallibrary.usc.edu. Excerpt from an anonymous individual.

Dr. Arenia C. Mallory Community Health Center. Retrieved from mallorychc.org/ www.acmallorychc.org/about-us.htm

Federal Register. 2013. Presidential Documents. *"Establishment of the Harriet Tubman Underground Railroad National Monument."* Volume 78, No. 60. Proclamation 8943, March 25, 2013

Fleming, S.A. (1995). *An answered prayer to a dream: Bethune-Cookman College 1904 – 1994.* Virginia Beach, VA: The Donning

Gardner, L. 2016, March 1). Retired HBCU presidents start search firm for black college leaders. The Chronicle of Higher Education. Retrieved from http://chronicle.com/article/ Retired-HBCU-Presidents-Start/235539?utm-source=HBCU

Ford, L.H. Letter to COGIC officials, March 4, 1991.

Goodson, G. 2016. *Rediscovering an American Classic: Essays on the Life of American Educator Dr. Arenia Conelia Mallory 1926 1976*

_____. 2015. *"The Church of God in Christ Transforms Women's Ministries Through the Positive Influence of Chief Apostle Bishop C.H. Mason."* Pp 73-96   In *With Signs Following: The Life and Ministry of Charles Harrison   Mason,* edited by Dr. Raynard Smith: COGIC Board of   Publication.

_____.2011 *Royalty Unveiled ROYALTY UNVEILED: Women Trailblazers in Church Of God In Christ International Missions*, HCM Publishing, Lancaster, TX, 36

Hall, D. (1990, June). The Whole Truth

Health Care Centers. Retrieved March 24, 2016 (mallorychc.com).

Hill, Elijah L., *Women Come Alive: Biography of Mother Lizzie Robinson 1865-1945*, Arlington, Texas: Perfecting the Kingdom International, 2005.

Holmes County Herald Archives. *"HONOR GUESTS at the Graduation of 300 Migrant Farmers Program."* December 1966. P. 7 Retrieved March 29, 2016 (http://hch.stparchive.com)
_____. *"COGIC to Honor Founder's Birthday."*
Retrieved March 23, 2016
(http://hch.stparchive.com)

_____. *"Doctor Mallory Honored For 50 Years."* Retrieved March 24, 2016
(http://hch.stparchive.com)

_____. *"Migrant Farmers Graduation Exercises to be held November 28."* November 24, 1966. P.7. Retrieved March 25, 2016 (http://hch.stparchive.com)

_____. *"Saints Dormitories Receive Financing from HUD."* Retrieved March 25, 2016 (http://hch.stparchive.com)

_____. *"Education Program to Begin Sept. 4."* August 30, 1973. Retrieved April 5,
2016 (http://hch.stparchive.com)

"Honoring the City of Lexington, Mississippi." Congressional
Record. www.congress.gov

Kiesel, Diane, *A Medical Pioneer in the Mississippi Delta*, Retrieved from TuftsNow, February 2, 2016 http://now.tufts.edu/articles/medical-pioneer-mississippi-delta

Lashley, E.M., *Glimpses Into the Life of a Great Mississippian and a Majestic American Educator, 1977* (Self Published)

Laughinhouse, Candace. 2011. *Discovering a Unique Female Resistance in Forerunners of Womanism: Dr. Arenia C. Mallory and Jo Ann Gibson Robinson* Women Studies in the History and Theology of the Church Professor: Dr. Estrelda Alexander January 25, 2011

Lincoln, C. Eric and Lawrence H. Mamiya. 1990. *The Black Church in the African American Experience*. Durham: Duke University Press.

Lovett, Leonard. 2003. "*Arenia Cornelia Mallory.*" Pp 859-860 in the New Dictionary of Pentecostal Charismatic Movements, edited by Stanley M. Burgess and Eduard M. Van Der Maas. Michigan: ZONDERVAN

Lynch, M. (2013, March 28). *Fostering diversity: A necessary step for hbcu survival*. Retrieved from http://diverseeducation.com/article/52261/

Phipps, William E. 2002. William Sheppard: Congo's African American Livingston/1st ed. Louisville, KY: Geneva Press

Piney Woods-*An Academic Oasis*, 60 Minutes with Morley Safer*http://www.cbsnews.com/news/piney-woods-an-academic-oasis/ http://www.digplanet.com/wiki/Piney_Woods_CountryLife_School*

Podesta, J. (2016, March 12). *Bethune Mary McLeod 1875 – 1955*. Contemporary Black Biography. Retrieved from Encyclopedia .com/doc/1G2-2870600013.htm

Raleigh, 1831 Act Passed by the General Assembly of the State of North Carolina at the Session of 1830—1831.

Sanders, Emma, *"A Call for Help from COGIC Liberia," The Whole Truth, Church of God In Christ*, Memphis, TN: Church of God in Christ, Inc., Volume 118, Number 7, November, 2014.

Simmons, Dovie M. and Olivia L. Martin. 1983. *Down Behind the Sun: The Story of Arenia Conelia Mallory.* Memphis, TN: Riverside Press.

Spruill, Michael Ray and Lee E. Van Zandt, *Mother Lizzie Robinson, The COGIC Matriarch And Her Two Daughters*, Preston, MD: Michael Ray Spruill, 2006.

The Whole Truth. N.d. *"Excerpt on Dr. Arenia C. Mallory."*

Tucker, A. (2009). *"Get the learnin' but don't lose the burnin' "The socio-cultural and religious politics of education in a black Pentecostal college.* Doctoral dissertation, Emory University. Retrieved from http://Search.Proquest.com/doc view/305094953

Ward, Tom. 2001. *"Medical Missionaries of the Delta: Dr. Dorothy Ferebee and the Mississippi Health Project."* Journal of Mississippi History 63: 189-203.

Watson, J. (2016, March 24). CMSI provides toolkit to assist HBCU presidents, *Diverse*, 33, (4), 3.

Williams, Heather *Self Taught: African American Education in Slavery and Freedom, 2005 The University of North Caroline Press*

Women's International Convention Church of God in Christ Souvenir Journal, Detroit, Michigan, May 7-12, 1957.

Wright, J. (2016, February). *Haynes champions the need for HBCUs.* Retrieved from http://www.afroo.com/haynes-champions-the-need-for-hbcus/#st hash.i6tlkvvk.dpuf

Wynveen, Brooklynn. 2009. *"Reasons For Use of Out-of-County Health Care Facilities in the Mississippi Delta."* The Review of Regional Studies 39: 213-225.

www.ingramcontent.com/pod-product-compliance
Lightning Source LLC
Chambersburg PA
CBHW070552160426
43199CB00014B/2466